The Call of the Child

The Call of the Child

Cultivating Peace in a Climate of Conflict

Bruce McKibben

Foreword by Gordon Hickson

RESOURCE *Publications* · Eugene, Oregon

THE CALL OF THE CHILD
Cultivating Peace in a Climate of Conflict

Copyright © 2021 Bruce McKibben. All rights reserved. Except for brief quotations in critical publications or reviews, no part of this book may be reproduced in any manner without prior written permission from the publisher. Write: Permissions, Wipf and Stock Publishers, 199 W. 8th Ave., Suite 3, Eugene, OR 97401.

Resource Publications
An Imprint of Wipf and Stock Publishers
199 W. 8th Ave., Suite 3
Eugene, OR 97401

www.wipfandstock.com

PAPERBACK ISBN: 978-1-7252-9544-5
HARDCOVER ISBN: 978-1-7252-9543-8
EBOOK ISBN: 978-1-7252-9545-2

04/12/21

All scripture quotations, unless otherwise indicated, are taken from the Holy Bible, New International Version®, NIV®. Copyright ©1973, 1978, 1984, 2011 by Biblica, Inc.™ Used by permission of Zondervan. All rights reserved worldwide. www.zondervan.com The "NIV" and "New International Version" are trademarks registered in the United States Patent and Trademark Office by Biblica, Inc.™

Scripture quotations marked NASB taken from the New American Standard Bible®, Copyright © 1960, 1962, 1963, 1968, 1971, 1972, 1973, 1975, 1977, 1995 by The Lockman Foundation. Used by permission. (www.Lockman.org)

Scripture quotations marked The Message taken from The Message. Copyright © 1993, 1994,1995,1996,2000,2001,2002. Used by permission of NavPress Publishing Group.

Scripture quotations marked NEB taken from the New English Bible, copyright © Cambridge University Press and Oxford University Press 1961, 1970. All rights reserved.

Scripture quotations marked TPT are from The Passion Translation®. Copyright © 2017, 2018 by Passion & Fire Ministries, Inc. Used by permission. All rights reserved. thePassionTranslation.com

Contents

Foreword by Gordon Hickson | vii
Acknowledgments | ix
Introduction | xi

The Heart of the Child | 1
1. The Great Shift | 3
2. A Murderer from the Beginning | 18
3. You Are What You Eat | 26
4. A Culture of Freedom | 44

The Walk of the Child | 51
5. What is Peace? | 53
6. Freedom from the Political Spirit | 60
7. Freedom from War | 70
8. Freedom from Violence and Criminality | 84
9. Economic Security | 97
10. Freedom from Lies, Deception and Accusation | 105
11. Freedom from Demonic Influences | 112
12. Freedom from Conflict | 119
13. Freedom from Worry | 128
14. A Haven of Blessing and Rest | 133
15. True Identity | 140
16. Health and Strength | 146
17. The Tangible Presence of God | 151

Conclusion | 156
Bibliography | 163

Foreword

IT IS A REAL honor to be asked to write a foreword for this book. We have loved getting to know Bruce and his family over the many years we have ministered in Churches in Norway, and particularly in Bergen. Over these years we have watched the ebb and flow of the unity and prayer movement, recognizing the incredible gift of peacemakers in this city, and how a city of peace can influence a whole nation.

When I first received this manuscript, my attention was seized within the first few pages: I realized that the whole essence of this book—The Call of the Child—centers around God's passion for us all to be these "peacemakers." Now that had me hooked, as my lifelong passion has been for peacemaking and reconciliation, often ministering under the name of Peacemakers, with the strap line of "together let's do the impossible!"

Bruce has been so thorough in searching through the Bible to discover and unpack this core purpose of God for each of our lives. He has pursued this with real honesty, humility and vulnerability: He really brings a clarity to the whole biblical battleground between those who have succumbed to the religion of the Tree of the Knowledge of Good and Evil and those who have chosen the inner peace of living and eating of the Tree of Life—our precious Jesus. This unveils the emptiness and deception of religion contrasted with the beauty of the child-like simplicity of trusting Jesus in everything.

In this year of the global pandemic, everything that can be shaken, has been shaken. Over this year, old religious wineskins have cracked and God has challenged so many of our religious beliefs. Bruce examines some of the significant areas of our lives in which the Holy Spirit enables us to live in freedom and victory—freedom from fears and anxiety, conflicts, lies, deceptions and accusations, as well as freedom from the demonic influences which rob us of our peace and economic security. Ultimately our pursuit

Foreword

of being "peacemakers" delivers us from the political spirits which drive us personally and nationally into war, violence and criminality.

As Paul shouts from the rooftops in his letter to the Ephesians, "Jesus is our Peace!" Through the Cross he has broken down every dividing wall of hostility which keeps us apart from each other. This peace not only bonds together formerly hostile people into the unity of the Spirit, but also fuses us together stronger than we ever imagined—just as a broken bone becomes stronger along the line of the break when it heals.

In this time of history when there is so much fragmentation and division, this book is a welcome clarion call for each of us as believers to host the very presence of God in our lives and homes, so that we can be the peacemakers for our families, communities and nations.

Rev Gordon Hickson
Oxford

Acknowledgments

I am thankful...

To my wife, Ellen, whose insights have germinated numerous ideas expressed in this book. Whose lifestyle is the embodiment of peace, generosity and hospitality. And whose attention to detail has greatly enhanced the quality of this text.

To Nathan Yake, who took time amidst the sleepless nights of early fatherhood to read an early draft of this book and challenge me, on many points, with thoughtful and well-reasoned opposing views. I probably haven't changed as much as he might have liked. But his contribution has been of great value to me and undoubtedly to the reader as well.

To Ann Anderson, Kjell-Morten Bratsberg Thorsen, Esther Kienast, Lilly Wenche Lie, Amy Petersen, and Mark Zastrow for their encouraging feedback and insights.

To the many preachers, teachers and authors whose wisdom has influenced who I am, and consequently what I have written, including: Jack Benson, Arthur Burk, Oswald Chambers, Trevor Galpin, Stephen Hill, Bill Johnson, James Jordan, Pelle Karlsson, Rhonda Hughey Mathisen, Ron Sider, Danny Silk, Ed Silvoso and Kris Vallotton.

Introduction

FATHER GOD. THE IMPLICATIONS of those two words are huge. And yet, I feel as though I have just begun the journey of experiencing God as Father; and consequently, who I am as his child.

Most of us believe that God is our Father. And yet we may find ourselves continuing to live our lives with a degree of servant, slave, or orphan behavior—rather than living out our lives in the royalty of a son or daughter of the Great King.

What is it that gets in the way of living out our calling? What keeps us from walking in the fullness of this revelation of God as a Good Father?

Jesus, in what is perhaps his best known teaching, started out with a bunch of poetic statements. We've heard them, but they are a bit lofty so we can be quick to overlook them in the practicalities of living life. One of these statements, I believe, holds a key to opening our hearts to this revelation of Father God:

> Blessed are the peacemakers, for they will be called children of God. (Matt 5:9)

In other words, cultivating the heart of a peacemaker increases our ability to experience God as a Good Father and to walk into the realm of sonship (or daughtership)[1] for which we were created. I don't mean that we need to gain more knowledge about peace or peacemaking. Rather, we need to experience a revelation of the heart of the Prince of Peace. A revelation that reaches deep into our own hearts and changes us to be more like Father God. This is The Call of the Child.

---

1. In this book, I am using the word sonship, as a gender-neutral term. It applies to both sons and daughters. The Norwegian language has a good word for this, *barnekår*; something which I miss in English.

Introduction

I use the verb *cultivating*, because becoming a peacemaker is a process of growth. If you read this book as a bunch of stuff you must do in order to be a peacemaker, then you have missed the point. Father God is our source. It all begins with him and flows from him. The Call of the Child is not a call for striving to be a peacemaker. Rather, it is a call to become so wrapped up in the love which flows from Father's heart that we become peacemakers.

The goal of this book is to take a deep look at what it means to be a peacemaker; and consequently what it looks like to live as children of our Good Father. I say that because true sons and daughters reflect the personality of their father. Or, as Jesus put it:

> You have heard that it was said, "Love your neighbor and hate your enemy." But I tell you, love your enemies and pray for those who persecute you, that you may be children of your Father in heaven. He causes his sun to rise on the evil and the good, and sends rain on the righteous and the unrighteous. (Matt 5:43–45)

Take some time to chew on that statement. Jesus is *not* saying here that you must love your enemies in order for the Father to accept you as his children. The Greek word *ginomai* (in the phrase ". . . that you may be children . . .") which is translated "you may be" could rather be translated "you show yourselves to be" or perhaps even "you be revealed as." The main point here is that our Good Father loves and blesses all people, even those who behave as enemies, who are evil, or who walk in unrighteousness. And that revelation will also shine forth in the way his mature sons and daughters live out their lives.

Loving your enemies is just one example of the nature of the God of Peace. In the first part of this book we will look at several aspects of his nature, before turning (in the second part of the book) to more concrete applications of living with the heart of a peacemaker.

But first a couple of disclaimers.

Anger

This is a book about peace. It is totally *not* my intention that this book should lead to strife or conflict. My desire is to see the Kingdom of Heaven, which is a kingdom of peace, increase in our communities in our time. But the "prince of this world" does not like peace, and he works hard to make it seem natural for us to think that the ways of peace are foolish or weak or

Introduction

undesirable or will steal our freedom; or whatever. And in that context we might just be angered by ideas which are different from what we have been led to believe.

James wrote that "the anger of man does not achieve the righteousness of God."[2] Which, to me, means that when I feel angry I need to stop and take an honest look at what will be achieved by my acting in anger. I have yet to experience that (either myself or anyone I know) following the path of anger has led to a good result.

Some of what I have written in this book is not politically correct. Striving to be politically correct is *not* a path to peace. True peace is found in the Kingdom of Heaven, and that Kingdom is seldom politically correct in the eyes of the kingdoms of this world. So, if I have written something which you find offensive, I haven't done so to offend you. I have tried to touch on difficult topics in a sensitive and honoring manner. But I might not, from your perspective, have succeeded. In which case, I apologize. My heart is to present peace; but sometimes the road to peace may need to expose and dislodge cherished lies.

One of the challenges when writing a book of this sort, is that there will be readers who may find my interpretations of scripture to be in conflict with their understanding. This could be because my presentation is incomplete, unbalanced or confusing. Or it could be because the reader feels bound to a particular understanding and is thereby not disposed to seeing things from a different perspective than they have previously done.

So let it be said that my intention is to be true to the Word of God from a theologically mainstream point of view. However, in my desire to pursue the heart of the God of Peace, there are many areas where I have been led to change the way I think. So there may well be things I have written in this book which might seem to be in conflict with your beliefs.

The Word of God is living and active. It is not meant to be interpreted only as a book of instructions or rules. Rather, it is best interpreted in living fellowship with the Spirit who inhabits the Word. Which means that it may at times appear to be in conflict with itself, when seen apart from the Holy Spirit's guidance.

The peacemaker is not called to criticize. In fact, none of us are called to be guardians of the truth.[3] Those who do so are operating under the influence of the Pharisaical spirit. The Pharisees accused Jesus of violating

---

2. Jas 1:20 NASB
3. See Romans 14:4 and James 4:11–12

Introduction

the law, of being soft on sin, of being too free, and of thinking too highly of himself. They condemned the Word of God for violating the Word of God; because the Pharisaical spirit so blinded them that the Word appeared to be in conflict with himself. But he wasn't.

If you don't like what I have written, please don't respond in anger. I welcome your reasoned feedback. It would please me if you contact me directly (at https://vandre.barbeint.no) rather than criticizing me in public fora.[4] We may not come to agreement. But I promise to respond honorably and peaceably. And I hope you will do likewise.

America Bashing

This is also a book about the heart of Father God and the culture of his Kingdom. It is my desire to write from a Kingdom of Heaven perspective. However, the cultures of this world are *very* different from the culture of the Kingdom. Any look at the subject of peace will necessarily involve touching on politics and culture, and thereby challenge some beliefs which we may hold dear.

I am an American; the son of a military officer. During my childhood we lived in several different states. The first of my forefathers who came to the shores of America (in 1620) were refugees fleeing religious persecution. I am also married to a Norwegian and have lived about half of my life in Norway.

Therefore, I know the American and Norwegian cultures better than those of other nations. And, not surprisingly, my observations will be to some degree biased by my immersion in these two cultures.

I am proud to be an American, but I am not necessarily proud of everything that my nation does or has done. I am a little bit wary of making such a statement, since one of the cultural doctrines that I grew up with was the idea of "My country, right or wrong." However, that is *not* a Kingdom of Heaven doctrine.

One of the characteristics of American culture is that (generalizing greatly) Americans tend to view most issues in black and white. You are either right or wrong, good or bad, for me or against me, and so on. The result is that if I point out some areas where American behavior, politics or traditions may not be conducive to peace, an American reader might be quick to interpret my statements as America bashing. That is absolutely *not* my intent.

---

4. You won't find me on facebook or other public debate fora. My experience is that those are all too seldom peaceful environments for reasoned discourse.

Introduction

There are ideals which we hold dear, and which we may perceive as being almost holy, and yet they can actually be in conflict with the culture of the Kingdom of Heaven. For example, the American Constitution and Declaration of Independence are documents which many Americans treat as almost sacred. However, it is important to remember that, even though to a large degree penned by men of faith, they are *not* inspired scripture. As good as those documents are, they are not perfect and they fall short of representing the ideal culture of mankind from a Kingdom of Heaven perspective. There are some areas where they may even be in opposition to Kingdom values.

You may find that challenging. Or it might even make you angry if I claim that some cherished aspect of your culture is at cross purposes with the Kingdom of Heaven. If so, then you should stop and think about what is going on.

We need a revelation of the heart of the Prince of Peace that reaches deep into our own hearts and changes us to be more like Father God. That will inevitably involve reassessing some of the aspects of our culture and lifestyle which we may not previously have questioned and which we might actually hold dear.

The Heart of the Child

Embracing the Heart of the Father

I have told you these things, so that in me you may have peace.
In this world you will have trouble. But take heart!
I have overcome the world.

(JOHN 16:33)

1

The Great Shift

According to Mark, Jesus began his public ministry with the following statement: "The kingdom of God is near. Repent and believe the good news."[1] You have perhaps heard these words so many times that you might not see just how truly radical this proclamation is; which outlined the purpose and direction of Jesus' activities for the next three years or so. So let's take a closer look.

The kingdom of God is near: For his listeners, this may have seemed kind of odd. Most likely, when they heard the word kingdom they were thinking in terms of a political or cultural kingdom. They probably thought they were already living in the kingdom of God. After all, they were God's chosen people, living within the boundaries of the kingdom of Judah. True, their kingdom was under the oppressive control of their Roman conquerors. So perhaps they thought that when Jesus talked about "is near" he was referring to a coming revolution which would throw off the oppressors. In a sense He was, but (as we shall see later) in a totally different manner than they would have thought.

Today, we understand that Jesus was not talking about a physical or political kingdom at all. He was talking about a spiritual kingdom where the culture of Heaven abounds. He was talking about spiritual realities that were about to be released into our physical world through the atoning sacrifice of himself.

Repent and believe: To repent is to turn around; to make a total change. You have perhaps heard the word used so many times in evangelical

---

1. Mark 1:15

appeals, that your first thought is that to repent means to stop sinning and start behaving righteously. While this is true, the term encompasses much more. It involves seeing things from a new perspective. It means that some cherished beliefs or doctrines or "truths" need to end up on the ash heap. To repent is to change the way you think.

If repenting is changing the way you think, then repenting and believing involves changing how you go about framing your system of trust. Belief is much more than accepting and acknowledging a system of understanding or knowledge. To believe is to trust. Your actual belief system will demonstrate itself through what you expect to happen, who and what has influence in your daily life, and how you react to things that are out of your control. If you are in the habit of only feeling secure when you think you are in control of your environment, then you would do well to change the way you trust.

Good news: Jesus spoke these words into a culture based on the Law of Moses. Although the Law is a good thing, after so many generations the culture had become very legalistic and the God of the Law seemed distant and angry. The idea of God coming near—a God who appears to be angry about our failure to follow his rules—doesn't sound very much like good news to me. Although a central aspect of the good news is that Jesus has paid the price for our sin, I believe that much of what is good about the good news is found in seeing God as a good, good Father rather than as an angry Judge.

What Happened on the Cross?

So, in essence, Jesus started his public ministry by proclaiming that something really good was close at hand. He then spent three years doing good things for and with common people. Things like: hanging out with them, healing them, setting them free, and treating them honorably. But he did these things in a way which made the political and religious leaders of his day uncomfortable, so they set out to have him killed.

Jesus was God in the flesh. He came on purpose to lay down his life as a sacrifice for the sin of all mankind. When he died on the cross, the entire penalty was paid. Or as Paul wrote to the Colossians, he nailed the certificate of debt that was against us to the cross: Paid in full.[2]

---

2. See Col 2:14

The Great Shift

Now, you have probably heard (more than once) that the wrath of God is against wickedness, that all have sinned and that the wages of sin is death.[3] But Paul told the Colossians that the death of Jesus on the cross was completely sufficient to satisfy all of the wrath of God.

Think about that. The wrath of God is satisfied. If that is really true, then there is nothing left for God to be angry about toward any human.

Which may leave you thinking: "Wait a minute. What about Hitler? Or terrorists or rapists or petty criminals? Does that mean God thinks those things are OK?"

No. Godlessness and unrighteousness have their price. Such things are *not* OK. But now that the penalty has been paid, what remains is no longer wrath, but the Father's intense longing that his emancipated children would acknowledge the freedom which is available to them and then walk into it.

Although the Bible carries a couple of hundred references to the wrath of God, that wrath is not primarily directed at people (whether good or bad). The lake of fire described in the book of Revelation was prepared for the devil and his angels,[4] who are the primary objects of the wrath of God. For his wrath is kindled against unrighteousness. Transgressions against his law bring wrath—not so much against the transgressor as against the transgression. As we shall see in chapter 3, these transgressions have their root in the knowledge of good and evil. The death of Jesus cleared away the object of that wrath,[5] so that we once again become able to see the true nature of God: a loving Father rather than an angry Judge.

For those who have put their trust in Jesus, there is no condemnation.[6] Instead, grace reigns. And grace means that every sin, mistake, and failure that you have done, or may yet come to do, is met with forgiveness—because the penalty has already been paid. Rather than looking to punish you, the Father is inviting you to be better acquainted with his nature and his ways, so that it becomes unnatural for you to do any of the things that might displease him.

For those who have not (yet) put their trust in Jesus, the situation is only slightly different. Though they may not acknowledge what Jesus accomplished for them on the Cross, the death of Jesus has still paid the entire

---

3. See Rom 1:18, 3:23 and 6:23. It is unfortunately all too common that people quote verse 3:23 (all have sinned) while overlooking verse 3:24 (all are justified freely by his grace).

4. See also Matt 25:41

5. See Rom 4:15

6. See Rom 8:1

penalty.[7] There is, therefore, no need or place for God to be angry with unbelievers. And there is no call for punishment, because perfect Love casts out all fear.[8]

That last paragraph may leave you wondering: What about the severity (or sternness) of God, as Paul wrote in Romans 11:22? Can we really say that God is not angry if his severity remains? I would say yes.

The Greek word *apotomia*, translated as *severity* (KJV and NASB) or *sternness* (NIV), is found only in this one verse of the bible. Literally, it means something that is abrupt or cut off, like a cliff. The word does not actually imply punishment, but it does imply separation and/or finality.

The parable of the prodigal son in Luke 15 gives an example of this severity. When the younger son chooses to take out his inheritance and start a life on his own, away from his true father, the father allows him to do so. In the time that he was away, his father considered him to be dead. In essence, he was cut off (*apotomia*). The father was hurt and heartbroken, but he was not angry and he never moved to enact punishment. It was the brother who demonstrated anger and a desire for punishment, something which was definitely not in alignment with his father's heart.

I might also point out that Jesus told the parable of the prodigal son specifically because some religious leaders had criticized him for associating with unholy people. The story is intended to demonstrate how Father God truly feels about, and relates to, people who choose disobedience and rebellion.

Children

And yet you may still wonder if this can really be true. Sure, it applies to the children of God. But can it really also apply to those on the outside? Which leads to a question of definition. Are we only God's children *after* we have believed?

In his letters to Rome, Galatia and Ephesus, Paul wrote about us being adopted to sonship. This English translation of the Greek word *huiothesia* is somewhat misleading. When translated as *adoption* it implies to us that we were not the Father's children until *after* we were adopted. But the Greek

---

7. See 1 John 2:2

8. See 1 John 4:18. Although there remains a judgment at the end of the age for those whose names are not found in the Book of Life (Rev 20:12–15), our God of grace and love is actually not out to punish sin prior to that time.

word does not mean that at all. The word actually refers to the act of *placing a son*. In the Roman context, that would be something more like a coming of age ceremony, or a proclamation that a son is fully the legal and rightful representative of his father. The point here is that we have always been the children of Father God. We were stolen, but the Cross has redeemed us and purchased us back from captivity. Those who have not seen or accepted this redemption are still children of God. They may still be "cut off," but Father is not angry with them and does not want to see them punished. No good father desires to see his child lost, even though the child may be disobedient.

This Good News is so radical and fundamental that it deserves re-iterating: The atoning sacrifice of Jesus on the Cross has completely paid the punishment for all sin—past, present, and future. The wrath of God is completely satisfied. There is no anger there. The Kingdom of God is near, and that is really Good News—but you may need to change the way you think about the nature of God in order to continue walking into the fullness of this revelation.

Natural Disasters

You may have encountered a tendency to look at natural disasters as signs of God's punishment. We might, for example, have heard some preacher proclaim that a recent earthquake, or a coming storm, or some such thing is a sign of God's great displeasure over some collective sin, such as abortion in the land.

I once read a book that took this idea to the extreme. The author's central claim was that the terribly destructive New England hurricane in September of 1938 was God's punishment for the Anglo-French acceptance of Hitler's annexation of Sudetenland[9] (a process in which the United States played no direct part), which contributed to enabling the Holocaust of World War II. This author then went on to present a long list of bad things that have happened since that time, and which coincided with events or actions that he felt violated God's will.

It is possible to build a case, through a selective reading of the Old Testament, that God deals with nations and peoples in such an arbitrarily vindictive manner. However, I do not believe that this is a true representation

---

9. A German-speaking region of Czechoslovakia. This acceptance (and the so-called Munich Betrayal a few days later) is a tragic example of the international politics which failed to restrain Hitler's regime in the months leading up to World War II.

of our God's nature. Would he really kill hundreds and destroy the homes of thousands in New England as a sign of his displeasure over coming political developments in Europe? Is it his habit to kill hundreds or thousands in an earthquake in order to demonstrate his displeasure over the killing of children in the womb? It may have looked as though he sometimes did so—before The Great Shift.

Jesus, however, paints a different picture. On one occasion, he referred to eighteen people who had been killed when a tower collapsed on them,[10] and said that the accident did *not* happen because of their guilt. In other words, he said that even though everyone is guilty, that doesn't mean that accidents or natural disasters come about as a punishment for that guilt. Such things are not acts of God.

Once again, Jesus is saying that the Kingdom is near, but we will need to change our understanding of who God is, in order to truly comprehend this Good News. In the Sermon on the Mount, Jesus portrayed his Father's good nature even more clearly:

> You have heard that it was said, "Love your neighbor and hate your enemy." But I tell you, love your enemies and pray for those who persecute you, that you may be children of your Father in heaven. He causes his sun to rise on the evil and the good, and sends rain on the righteous and the unrighteous. If you love those who love you, what reward will you get? (Matt 5:43–46a)

It is the nature of the Father to bless people whether they deserve it or not; and to love people regardless of whether or not they love him.

Now, I have spent the majority of my life living in rainy climates. So when I read that he sends rain on the righteous and the unrighteous, I need to remind myself that rain is a blessing rather than a punishment. Jesus was speaking to an agricultural society in a desert climate. For them, rain is a huge blessing. And Jesus says that it is his Father's nature to intentionally bless people with good things, regardless of how righteous they may be.

That might leave you wondering: If God is not out to punish, then why do accidents and natural disasters happen? I don't have an answer to that question. But I do see a pattern.

After sin entered the world, the earth was cursed, and the earth longs to be set free from that curse.[11] This curse means that the earth does not function as it was originally intended. In the absence of great effort, it

---

10. See Luke 13:4
11. See Gen 3:17 and Rom 8:19–22

produces thorns and thistles rather than trees pleasing to the eye and good for food. Natural disasters are the fruit of this curse. And, sadly, many people throughout the world live their lives in this realm of curse.

It is possible to step up from the level of the curse to the level of sowing and reaping. By this, I mean that it is possible to live our lives by following the rules (God's Law) and thereby gain the benefits of following those rules. But, at the same time, to the extent that we fail to follow the rules, we also become subject to the consequences of breaking the rules.

However, I do not believe that Father God wants us to live at either of those two levels. There is a third level: the level of blessing. Those who live their lives in the realm of blessing are filled with peace. They have nothing to fear. They have no worries. Just as the psalmist, they can say "Surely your goodness and love will follow me all the days of my life."[12] The key to living a life of blessing is learning to walk in the love of the Father—a perfect love in which there is no fear and no punishment. We'll look more closely at this Tree of Life in chapter 3.

A Very Brief History of Punishment

As you read through the Old Testament, you could draw the conclusion that God's relation to mankind has to some degree been framed by a need to punish sin. So let's take a look at that.

Adam

> To the woman he said, "I will make your pains in childbearing very severe; with painful labor you will give birth to children. Your desire will be for your husband, and he will rule over you."
> To Adam he said, "Because you listened to your wife and ate fruit from the tree about which I commanded you, 'You must not eat from it,' cursed is the ground because of you; through painful toil you will eat food from it all the days of your life. It will produce thorns and thistles for you, and you will eat the plants of the field. By the sweat of your brow you will eat your food until you return to the ground, since from it you were taken; for dust you are and to dust you shall return." (Gen 3:16–19)

---

12. Ps 23:6

The Heart of the Child

In Genesis 3, we read the tragic story of the first time that a human sinned. The commandment was to not eat of a specific tree. The verses above outline the consequences of breaking that commandment; which reach into nearly every aspect of human life to this day. But they are consequences. They are *not* punishment.

God very specifically cursed, and thereby punished, the serpent. But, to the woman and the man he described the consequences of their actions. Those consequences spring out of their broken relationship with God, leading to the loss of fullness of life. Thus death entered into the human race as a consequence of the loss of contact with the Author of Life.

The fundamental consequence for Adam, and the tendency for men in general even to this day, is the futile attempt to find fulfillment in what we do. The knowledge of good and evil gives us the illusion that our accomplishments, our reputation or the work of our hands will satisfy the longing for love, intimacy and acceptance for which we were created. It is a poor substitute: we may toil and labor, but our labors will fail to produce what our hearts truly long for.

Similar is the consequence for the woman: "Your desire will be for your husband, and he will rule over you." This is not an expression of God's intent nor of his divine order.[13] Rather, it is a description of how womankind, in their longing for the intimacy of relationship they were designed to have with their creator, will tend to look for that to be fulfilled in relationship with a man. And how that longing could dominate them, even to their own destruction.

Our efforts to find substitutes for the intimate relationship with Father God, that was broken by the fall, weary us until our lives wear out and we return to dust. Father God grieves over that loss even more than his creation does. He heart has never been for punishment, but for restoration.

Cain

In the very next generation, death began to manifest itself. Cain murdered his brother. Murder was at that time something which the human race had never experienced. As shocking as this event was, God did not punish Cain

---

13. The phrase, "I will make your pains in childbearing severe," could possibly be interpreted as a punishment. I don't claim to have a lot of insight into that. But my wife points out the value of that pain in strengthening the bond between mother and child.

with death. Cain fell under a curse and was driven from the land that had been his delight. But his violence was not punished with violence.

Noah

Wickedness increased to the point where the earth was corrupt and full of violence. The heart of the Lord was deeply troubled over how things had turned out, and he was compelled to do something about it.[14] This is the first record we have of God actively moving to bring about the death of a person as a consequence of their sin. But it is also the first record of God entering into a covenant with a human.

Prior to Noah, the only allusion to a covenant is the covenant of marriage.[15] And I think there is a parallel in God's covenant with Noah. For in the midst of the punishment of the entire human race, God (by his own initiative) establishes a covenant of love and provision forever.

We know very little about what mankind was like in the time before Noah entered the ark. The description of the wickedness of that age, "that every inclination of the thoughts of the human heart was only evil all the time,"[16] is total. And this was only the tenth generation after Adam. Hundreds of generations have passed since the time of Noah, which leads me to wonder: is the wickedness of our day worse (in the sight of God) than the wickedness before Noah's time? I think not, because at the birth of Jesus, the angels sang that God is pleased with mankind;[17] and since that time the presence of the Holy Spirit in the people of God has been influencing societies for the better.

Abraham

In the tenth generation after Noah, God initiated a new covenant with Abraham. This covenant does not eradicate the covenant of survival that God made with Noah and all of his descendants. But this new covenant goes further by establishing a friendship relationship. This friendship covenant

---

14. See Gen 6:5–13

15. Although marriage is not specifically referred to as covenant until much later, Jesus' statement in Matt 19:5–6 clearly implies that God has always considered marriage to be a covenant.

16. Gen 6:5

17. See Luke 2:14 NASB

is revealed through several encounters between God and Abraham during the course of his life. There are especially two of these encounters that give insight into how God relates to punishment. We'll look at those shortly.

I have encountered teaching which interprets some of Abram's/Abraham's actions as being contrary to God's will. God told Abram to leave his relatives, but Abram took his nephew Lot with him. Genesis 13 tells us that the men of Sodom, where Lot eventually chose to settle, were sinning greatly. In Genesis 14 we read about how Sodom (and Lot) were plundered and captured by the army of four kings, and how Abram and 318 men routed them and rescued Lot. Fifteen or twenty years later, God meets Abraham on his way to punish Sodom for its wickedness, but Abraham tries to talk him out of it.

One might interpret all of this as Abraham standing in the way of God's will. If God is primarily a holy judge who demands obedience, it could be said that Abram disobeyed the Lord by letting Lot go with him, and that he messed up God's intended punishment of Sodom the first time around, and nearly messed it up the second time around with his manipulative whining to try and save his nephew.

But I see things differently. I believe that God, through his many encounters with Abraham, is demonstrating that it is his nature to build relationship and friendship and blessing. At the same time he demonstrates that it is not his nature to demand obedience and to lash out with punishment when his demands are not met.

In one such encounter, God promises to give the land (where Abram is a wanderer) to Abram's descendants. But not yet:

> In the fourth generation your descendants will come back here,
> for the sin of the Amorites has not yet reached its full measure.
> (Gen 15:16)

There is an astonishing principle in this verse. In essence, God is telling Abram, "I am going to give you all of this land, but I can't give it to you yet, because the people who now dwell there have not yet sinned so much that I am compelled to rid the land of them." The implication here is that there is a threshold of wickedness which must be crossed before our God will intervene with punishment. The consequence was that Abraham's descendants would spend hundreds of years waiting and enduring slavery. Even the friendship between God and Abraham was not enough for God to punish the inhabitants of the land before it was unavoidable.

The Great Shift

One afternoon, several years later, Abraham was resting by his tent when three visitors dropped by. These visitors, the Lord God and two angels, were actually on their way to investigate if the sin was so grievous as the "outcry against Sodom and Gomorrah"[18] appeared to be. In other words, they were going to determine if the threshold of wickedness had been crossed. But before doing so, they chose to drop in on Abraham. The reason that God chose to first eat lunch with his friend can be seen in this statement:

> Then the LORD said, "Shall I hide from Abraham what I am about to do? Abraham will surely become a great and powerful nation, and all nations on earth will be blessed through him. For I have chosen him, so that he will direct his children and his household after him to keep the way of the LORD by doing what is right and just, so that the LORD will bring about for Abraham what he has promised him." (Gen 18:17–19)

God had chosen Abraham to be a source of blessing to all nations; inviting him to be the patriarch of a culture of righteousness and justice that would walk in the way of the Lord. And so, before investigating the situation in Sodom and Gomorrah, the Lord wanted to talk it over with his friend. Could it be that God was hoping Abraham would convince him to choose mercy rather than judgment?

Abraham rose to the occasion. He appealed to the nature of his Friend: "It's not like you to punish without cause." Perhaps Abraham remembered the prophecy over his own descendants, how they would wait hundreds of years for their promised inheritance, because the Lord is slow to anger.

In any case, Abraham extracted a promise from the Lord that there would be no punishment if only ten righteous people were found among them. As it turned out, only four people were found and they were evacuated from the area before the cities were destroyed. Could Abraham have gotten God to withhold his judgment for the sake of only one person? Perhaps. For our God has no pleasure in the death of the wicked.[19]

Moses

Fast forward about 400 years. The descendants of Abraham have become slaves in Egypt, but God remembers his covenant with Abraham, and

---

18. See Gen 18:20–21
19. See Ezek 18:23, 33:11

also sees that the sin of the Amorites is so grievous that it has crossed the threshold for punishment. And then God punished the Amorites and gave the land to the descendants of Abraham.

> But be assured today that the LORD your God is the one who goes across ahead of you like a devouring fire. He will destroy them; he will subdue them before you. And you will drive them out and annihilate them quickly, as the LORD has promised you. After the LORD your God has driven them out before you, do not say to yourself, "The LORD has brought me here to take possession of this land because of my righteousness." No, it is on account of the wickedness of these nations that the LORD is going to drive them out before you. It is not because of your righteousness or your integrity that you are going in to take possession of their land; but on account of the wickedness of these nations, the LORD your God will drive them out before you, to accomplish what he swore to your fathers, to Abraham, Isaac and Jacob. (Deut 9:3–5)

God had raised up Moses and through him established a covenant with the descendants of Abraham.[20] The intent of this covenant is to be a covenant of love and intimacy, very much like a covenant of marriage. God chose to make this people his treasured possession. But the people were a nation of slaves, who were much more accustomed to following their master's instructions than relating to a Friend. So, rather than learning to know this awesome God, they asked to be told what to do.[21] And then God gave Moses the Law—a collection of rules, instructions, consequences, and punishments; many of which were punishable by death.

Although there are many good things about this Law, it is not perfect. It does not reflect the fullness of the nature of God nor does it accomplish the will of God.[22] If it did, there would have been no need for a new covenant.

In particular, the Law fell short because it is a system of rules for behavior that are enforced by punishment. That is a system which can work fairly well with slaves, but it is not a good system for raising up mature sons and daughters. And it cannot fulfill a covenant of love and intimacy.

---

20. See Exod 19:5–6 and Deut 29:12–13
21. See Exod 20:19
22. See Matt 19:7–8, Gal 3:19–22, Heb 7:11 and 7:18–19, and Jer 20:25

The Great Shift

Jesus

In the fullness of time, Jesus, the Son of God, was born while angels sang, "Glory to God in the highest, And on earth peace among men with whom He is pleased."[23] About thirty-three years later, this same Jesus was hung on a cross, bearing the punishment for all sin, for all mankind—past, present and future.

A new covenant was established—a covenant of grace and mercy, of peace and blessing, of life and abundance. And, more than any covenant before it, it is a marriage covenant. A covenant of love to reveal the bride of Christ. In this new covenant there is no place for punishment.

> There is no fear in love. But perfect love drives out fear, because fear has to do with punishment. (1 John 4:18)

Mercy Triumphs over Judgment

Even before he paid our penalty on the Cross, Jesus demonstrated this new covenant of grace. He fellowshipped with sinners, he healed and delivered people who did not deserve it, and he honored people regardless of their status.

Have you considered how truly remarkable that is?

Jesus is the Son of God, the image of the invisible God, the exact representation of God's being, in whom the fullness of the Deity lives.[24] Now, if our God is so holy that he cannot tolerate any form of sin in his presence, how could Jesus eat with sinners? If your picture of the nature of God is a judge who punishes sinners, then who was this Jesus that spent his three years of public ministry in Judea hanging out with some very unholy people?

Jesus said that he only did what he saw his Father doing, and he only spoke the words which his Father gave him to speak. If that is true, then God the Father also likes to hang out with sinners, heal and deliver people who don't deserve it, and honor them. Everything that Jesus did was an exact representation of the nature of his Father.

James, most likely the brother of Jesus, wrote in his letter that mercy triumphs over judgment.[25] If that is true, then judgment (and by implica-

---

23. Luke 2:14. Note the difference from how God felt about the people of Noah's time.
24. See Col 1:15 and 2:9, and Heb 1:3
25. See Jas 2:13

tion punishment) is an imperfect and inferior thing, which is defeated and disarmed by mercy.

Jesus demonstrated this one morning when a woman was dragged before him by a group of self-righteous men.[26] This woman had been caught in the act of committing adultery, a sin which according to the Law should be punished by stoning. They demanded that Jesus pass judgment, not so much because they wanted to kill the woman, but because they wanted to force Jesus to choose between his lifestyle of mercy and the demands of the Law.

Jesus, the exact representation of his Father, chose mercy. Not only did he choose mercy for the humiliated woman who had been thrown at his feet, but he also chose mercy for the judgmental men who wanted to see both the woman and Jesus condemned and punished for violating the Law.

And mercy led to peace. What had been an aggressive and destructive setting was transformed. The angry men left, one by one, without conflict or violence, until only the woman remained. Then Jesus blessed her.

This was not an isolated event, but a clear example of the nature of God, who *delights* to show mercy,[27] as demonstrated in the life of Jesus. Everything Jesus did was an expression of the Kingdom of God coming near. The Good News was that a Great Shift was taking place. The Law and its system of punishment for sin was about to be fulfilled by the ultimate act of mercy: That the entire punishment would be paid in full through the death of Jesus on the Cross.

On the other side of that Great Shift there would be peace. There would no longer be any need for judgment, for punishment, for violence, or for fear. Mercy would truly triumph over judgment.

This triumph over judgment is rooted in the core of the nature of our God. Perhaps the most dramatic revelation of God's nature came when Moses asked to see God in all his glory.

> And the LORD said, "I will cause all my goodness to pass in front of you, and I will proclaim my name, the LORD, in your presence. I will have mercy on whom I will have mercy, and I will have compassion on whom I will have compassion." (Exod 33:19)

And after passing by, covering Moses with his hand, and then revealing himself to Moses, God proclaimed his name:

---

26. See John 8:2–11
27. See Mic 7:18

The Great Shift

> Then the LORD came down in the cloud and stood there with him and proclaimed his name, the LORD. And he passed in front of Moses, proclaiming, "The LORD, the LORD, the compassionate and gracious God, slow to anger, abounding in love and faithfulness, maintaining love to thousands, and forgiving wickedness, rebellion and sin. Yet he does not leave the guilty unpunished; he punishes the children and their children for the sin of the parents to the third and fourth generation." (Exod 34:5–7)

At first glance, it might seem illogical that the LORD forgives wickedness, rebellion and sin; and yet does not leave the guilty unpunished. It wasn't until the LORD Himself laid down his own life on the Cross so that the guilty would not be left unpunished, that this revelation of the nature of God really began to make sense. All of creation is longing for this to be revealed.[28]

It took a little while for the disciples of Jesus to understand this Great Shift. There were several times that they thought they could help Jesus establish his kingdom by power, by might, or by violence. But that was not the way Jesus did things.

For example, on one occasion Jesus and his followers were rejected when they wanted to stop to rest in a village.[29] James and John thought that they could help Jesus out, after meeting such disrespect: "Shall we call down fire from heaven to destroy them?" However, Jesus rebuked them. That kind of judgment was not at all the way of his Father. And Jesus wanted his disciples to learn to not think that way either.

A similar thing happened in the garden when Jesus was arrested. One of the disciples took a sword and cut off someone's ear. But Jesus rebuked his disciples for resorting to violence.[30] In the midst of being arrested, he healed the ear which had been cut off. Mercy triumphs over judgment.

After Jesus was raised from the dead and the Holy Spirit was poured out on the believers, then they started to really grasp this Great Shift. We no longer see any record of them arguing over who was the greatest. We no longer see them having any desire to punish their enemies. And we see absolutely no examples in the new testament of believers acting violently. Rather, we see them praying for their persecutors, rejoicing over their sufferings, and overcoming evil with good.[31]

---

28. See Rom 8:19
29. See Luke 9:52–56
30. See Matt 26:51–52 and Luke 22:49–51
31. See Acts 5:41, 7:60, and Rom 12:17,21

2

A Murderer from the Beginning

Our God is a God of love. And in the beginning the Father, the Son, and the Spirit existed together in an intimate harmony of love and peace. They created various spiritual beings to share in their love. And eventually they created the physical world in which we humans live. At some point, either before or after the creation of the physical world, a rebellion took place and peace was broken. In order to understand true spiritual peacemaking, it may be helpful to take a closer look at how this came about.

Ezekiel, in a prophecy about the king of Tyre,[1] describes a spiritual being of unmatched beauty and power at some point in prehistory. This being was a guardian cherub; perhaps the highest ranking angel in the heavenlies. He is described as having been perfect in beauty and having held a special position and responsibility in the presence of God. But, despite his exalted position, he reached out for more:

> How you have fallen from heaven, morning star, son of the dawn! You have been cast down to the earth, you who once laid low the nations! You said in your heart, "I will ascend to the heavens; I will raise my throne above the stars of God; I will sit enthroned on the mount of assembly, on the utmost heights of Mount Zaphon. I will ascend above the tops of the clouds; I will make myself like the Most High." But you are brought down to the realm of the dead, to the depths of the pit. (Isa 14:12–15)

---

1. Ezek 28:12–17

A Murderer from the Beginning

This being is satan, the enemy. Jesus describes him as a murderer from the beginning and the father of lies.[2] Prior to the rebellion neither dishonesty nor death existed. It was the outbreak of these things that led to the breaking of peace.

The Bible doesn't tell us very much about how this rebellion came about, or when it took place. It looks as though the enemy took about a third of the angels with him, and that there was war between them and the remaining angels.[3] And the enemy has been cast down to the earth.

What can be difficult for us to understand, is the fact that even though the enemy has been totally defeated he is still in a position to steal, kill, and destroy. It would have taken no effort for God to simply annihilate the devil and eliminate his deception and destruction completely. And yet, in the wisdom of God, this has not happened.

I do not claim to understand why. But I believe that one facet of the explanation can be found in the death of Jesus on the Cross. Paul tells us[4] that the enemy was completely defeated when Jesus, the Son of the Living God, laid down his life on the Cross.

Looking back at Isaiah 14, we see that the enemy's rebellion was rooted in his ambition to conquer and win. The root issue was not the enemy's desire to be exalted or to rule or to be worshiped. Those are only symptoms. The root issue was the enemy's desire to conquer, to achieve by might, to overpower, to force his will.[5]

And so the Almighty God defeated this enemy through an amazing and seemingly foolish display of weakness. God became a man, and allowed himself to be ridiculed, tortured, and hung on a cross. And then God Almighty died. The Prince of Peace hanging naked and broken on the remains of a tree.

> For the foolishness of God is wiser than human wisdom, and the weakness of God is stronger than human strength. (1 Cor 1:25)

---

2. See John 8:44
3. See Rev 12:3–9
4. See Col 2:15
5. It could be said that the enemy's root issue was pride; which is simply another name for this desire to conquer and overpower.

Herein lies a fundamental difference between the realm of darkness and the Kingdom of God Almighty: The Principle of the Cross.[6] Simply put, this principle is: To lose is to win.

The greatest victory ever won throughout all history was won through the weakness demonstrated on the Cross. God at his weakest defeated and totally disarmed the strength of the enemy. This was no accident, but rather a pivotal example of how the Kingdom of Heaven operates. True victory is won through apparent weakness and loss.

Winning

The way of the murderer, the father of lies, is to win by might. He makes use of his strength, his corrupted wisdom, his persuasiveness, and his exceptional talent for deception and accusation in order to achieve his goals. He is forceful, demanding, controlling, manipulative, and devious. His appetite to succeed in his ambitions is insatiable.

There is nothing peaceful about this being, because at the core of his nature he is a murderer, a thief, and a deceiver. One of the ways he steals peace is through accusation. He accuses people of failing to meet the requirements of the Law and demands that every failure be punished. By so doing, he believes that he is forcing God to destroy the world which God so loves.

This enemy is consumed with power. He has no regard for freedom, even though he may call many things liberating—while they actually lead to bondage.

Every achievement attained through force, through strength of will, by control, or by limiting the freedom of others is rooted in the ways of evil. Whenever we set out to win or to succeed in this manner, we are actually operating in accordance with the ways of the enemy.[7]

Ever since the fall of man in the garden of Eden, the ways of this world have been dominated by the enemy's character. Therefore, it is common in

---

6. I am indebted to Pelle Karlsson and his book *Korsets Princip* for introducing me to this often overlooked treasure in the ways of God. Unfortunately, as far as I know, Karlsson's book has only been published in Swedish and Norwegian, and is no longer in print. I do cover this topic more fully in the middle section of my book, *Walking His Ways*.

7. Just to be clear: I am not saying that you are in league with the enemy if you play to win at basketball or a board game or such. But how you play the game *does* matter. Playing with competitive excellence is a very different thing from using whatever means may be available to conquer your opponent.

the cultures of this world to value strength, ambition and conquering. For the most part, those who rule and who influence society have gained their positions through the forceful defeat of their opponents. In other words, their achievements are gained through use of the same attitudes and methods that led to the fall of satan.

Jesus once said, "What people value highly is detestable in God's sight."[8] And he followed up with a strange statement: That people are forcing their way into the Kingdom. This was spoken in the context of exposing the condition of the hearts of the Pharisees, so I don't think that Jesus considered taking the Kingdom by force to be a good thing.[9] Taking something by force, by power, by cleverness, or the like, is operating with the mindset of the devil. It may well accomplish something in the here and now, but the eternal results will be negligible.

Losing

The way of God Almighty is to lay down his life. Peace can never be achieved by force, but only through freedom rooted in love. Love is much more than a fuzzy emotion or a good feeling.

> Love is patient, love is kind. It does not envy, it does not boast, it is not proud. It does not dishonor others, it is not self-seeking, it is not easily angered, it keeps no record of wrongs. Love does not delight in evil but rejoices with the truth. It always protects, always trusts, always hopes, always perseveres. (1 Cor 13:4–7)

From this description, love is all about giving—regardless of the response. There is a huge risk in love, because the person on the receiving end is free to reject or misuse that which is extended to them. It is not possible to truly love with an ambition of conquering.

And so, our God who is Love demonstrates his love through freedom. Although he loves every person, he does not force anyone to love him or to honor him or even to obey him. Although he is the omnipotent God Almighty, his creation is free to reject him. The result is that he appears to be a loser.

---

8. Luke 16:15. See also Rom 8:7, Jas 4:4, and 1 John 2:15–16

9. I am fully aware that there are also other valid interpretations of Luke 16:16. For example, we are called to actively pursue the Kingdom and its righteousness rather than to passively expect the Kingdom to materialize around us. But that is a different issue.

It may seem foolish, but choosing freedom rather than force has enormous value in the spiritual realm. Choosing grace rather than justice has the power to disarm the forces of darkness. For mercy triumphs over judgment.

Much of the Sermon on the Mount is about this principle in practice. From "blessed are the meek" to turning the other cheek to loving your enemies, the culture of the Kingdom of Heaven thrives in apparent loss.

> But I tell you, love your enemies and pray for those who persecute you, that you may be children of your Father in heaven. He causes his sun to rise on the evil and the good, and sends rain on the righteous and the unrighteous. (Matt 5:44–45)

Even in the face of great persecution, the children of Father God most frequently respond with forgiveness and peace. A careful look at how Christians who suffer persecution, both in the world today and throughout history, shows that they very rarely respond with violence.[10] And responding to hate with kindness frequently results in the oppressor's hearts opening up to repentance and salvation.

Standing

Now, you may be thinking something like, "Wait a minute. Isn't our God a mighty conqueror, the Lion of Judah?" Yes, indeed, he is. Countless times throughout the Old Testament our God is portrayed as a God of strength. I do not in any way mean to diminish that.

But, after The Great Shift, the situation has changed. The enemy was totally defeated and completely disarmed when our Mighty Warrior God laid down his own life on the Cross.[11] And from that time forward there is actually nothing left to defeat.

In Ephesians 6, Paul writes that our battle is against spiritual forces. And then he instructs us to put on the full armor of God. Have you noticed that the armor he describes is primarily defensive in nature? Even the sword of the Spirit is not primarily an attack weapon—the word translated as sword is not the word for a long battle sword, but rather the word for a dagger which, among other things, would be used to remove darts or

---

10. For example, see the University of Notre Dame report, *Under Caesar's Sword*, at https://ucs.nd.edu

11. See Col 2:15

arrows. Finally, after putting all of this armor on, Paul says to stand. He says neither attack nor charge. He says: Stand.

To stand is *not* to passively let the powers of darkness walk over us. It is a very active business. We are to stand firm in the truth, exposing lies and accusations to be powerless on account of the victory of the Cross. We are to take the wind out of the sails of attitudes and deceptions that would limit or obscure the knowledge of the Kingdom.[12] The simple act of resisting the devil will cause him to flee.[13]

One of the tactics of the enemy is to entice us into engaging with him. Unless you have a very clear leading from the Holy Spirit to move in a specific act of spiritual warfare, then attacking the enemy is a perilous venture. To attack is to move in the realm of winning. In so doing, you empower the enemy by accepting the lie that there is something in his realm which has not already been defeated.

As we stand against spiritual darkness, the primary weapon at hand is to speak truth in grace. Grace is not a weapon of attack, but it is the most powerful and effective weapon available to us for disarming powers of darkness. In fact, from a spiritual perspective, grace is a stealth weapon. Peter wrote that grace and the Messiah's suffering which released its glory are things into which angels long to look.[14] In other words, grace is an incomprehensible concept for angelic beings; the reality of which is hidden from the demonic realm.

It is the devil who attacks, and he loses if only we stand firm. Because, in the spiritual realm the victory is always won through weakness and never through strength. The place of peace is a place of safety.

Perfect Love Drives Out Fear

> There is no fear in love. But perfect love drives out fear, because fear has to do with punishment. The one who fears is not made perfect in love. (1 John 4:18)

The idea of losing might just seem frightening to you. Should we really let our enemies win? Should we really not move to defend ourselves? What about if someone threatens our loved ones?

12. See 2 Cor 10:5
13. See Jas 4:7
14. See 1 Pet 1:12

The Heart of the Child

These are reasonable questions, and they should not be pushed aside lightly. But these questions are rooted in fear. And the one who fears is not made perfect in love.

In my understanding, there are two kinds of fear:[15] the fear of death and the fear of losing control. Losing control encompasses shame, embarrassment, failure, inadequacy, lack, and the like, as well as sickness, injury, or suffering loss.

The fear of losing control is rooted in what I would call the orphan spirit. The orphan spirit tells us that we have to take responsibility for making sure that we have what we need in order to live. This idea is ingrained in us from the time that Adam ate the forbidden fruit, thereby separating us from Father God. And it is amplified by the degree that our parents have failed to protect and provide for us. The antidote to this kind of fear is trust. As we learn to trust that Father God, through his perfect love, really does provide for us, then we can be set free from the fear of losing control.

The fear of death is rooted in the idea of punishment. At some point after death, we will stand before our Maker in a place of judgment. If we believe that this place of judgment is a place of punishment, then there is every reason to fear. Praise be to God for The Great Shift. There is nothing left to punish for those who are made perfect in love.

The peacemaker can not walk in fear. Therefore, the peacemaker must walk in love. God is perfect love. Only a deep and thorough experience of unlimited trust in the God who laid down his own life as an expression of his love for our world will drive out the fear that would enslave us. Only a revelation of the caring and all-sufficient love of Father God will free us from the fear with which the orphan spirit seeks to enshroud us.

I know that this works.

On a hot summer day in 1985, I was on board a mid-sized four-engine jet aircraft. We were rolling down the runway at an airport near Los Angeles, California. This was a research flight, and the plan was for us to fly as far south along the coast of Mexico as possible before returning to Los Angeles, so the fuel tanks were full.

Just before take-off, a couple of tires blew out and disintegrated, which left the right-side undercarriage running on the metal rims at a speed of about 140 knots. The pilot threw on the brakes, and fortunately had plenty of runway ahead of him. But metal shards from the rims ripped a hole in

---

15. I am intentionally not looking at the fear of the Lord here, because that is an entirely different thing—which walks hand in hand with perfect love.

the bottom of the right wing. Fuel started to leak out and quickly caught fire. This was not a good situation. I had no control, and death was a very real possibility. Some said that it looked as though we were rolling down the runway in a ball of flame.

The plane came to a stop, and within about 30 seconds all of the 19 people on board had evacuated down the slides and run off into the grass to the left of the runway. When I turned around to look back, I saw sheets of flame pouring down from the far side of the aircraft. That's when it occurred to me that it was a good thing the plane had stopped on the runway and not in the midst of all that dry grass surrounding us. We stood there for quite some time watching as the plane was gutted by fire. But the only injury that day was a rug-burned elbow which my colleague got on his way down the slide.[16]

My strongest impression from that day was the complete lack of fear that I felt. As the brakes were on and the plane was shaking more than I had ever before experienced, I distinctly recall saying to the Lord something like: "Well, either we'll stop or we won't. I am in your hands." No fear. Just peace. I was in God's hands, and the outcome really didn't matter. In fact, this peace rested so strongly upon me that I recall being a little bit surprised by how shook up most of the other passengers were.

Do I go looking for those kinds of experiences? Absolutely not. But if they do turn up, I know that I know that I can trust my Father God regardless of the outcome. But what if I had died? Yes, what if?

To lose is to win.

---

16. There is a brief accident summary with photos at: https://aviation-safety.net/database/record.php?id=19850717-10

3
———

You Are What You Eat

One day when our daughter was in high school, she was telling me about her frustration with a classmate. This classmate had begun to change her lifestyle in the direction of drinking and partying. And it pained my daughter to see that happening.

Not only am I male, but I am also an engineer. So, rather than just listening to my daughter, I defaulted to giving some advice aimed at fixing the problem. But she cut me off and said, "Papa, you've got to understand. She has grown up in a typical Christian family where she had to follow rules. Not like us."

That stopped me in my tracks. I thought, "Huh? What have we done right here?"

I have often thought it was probably a good thing we've not been asked to teach on raising children. Although we have raised three, and things have turned out well with all of them, it's not been easy to say what we have done right. It is only within recent years that I have discovered a vocabulary to describe what my daughter referred to that day.

This chapter explores that paradigm. We have apparently been living it, at least to some degree, as our children have grown. And yet, putting it into words has increased its impact in my life. It has to do with what we eat. And it begins in a garden.

The Garden

Genesis 2–3 tells the story of the fall of man—when peace in the physical realm was broken and death entered into the human experience. This happened in the Garden of Eden, the dwelling place of the Man and the Woman whom The Lord God had created. It was a place of peace. Father God created people to live in loving relationship with himself, and gave them a home ideally suited for that relationship to flourish.

In the garden were all kinds of trees, pleasing to the eyes and good for food. In addition there were two trees which, by their description, were of a different nature[1] than the other trees. One was the Tree of Life and the other was the Tree of Knowledge of Good and Evil.[2] Apparently, eating from either of these two trees was not simply a matter of gaining physical nourishment, but rather an impartation of spiritual perspective and understanding.

The Man was expressly forbidden to eat of the Tree of Knowledge of Good and Evil. But no such restriction appears to have been placed on eating from the Tree of Life. I believe that, among other things, these two trees represent two streams of thought, or two kinds of wisdom, which stand in opposition to one another. In the garden, the Man and Woman could partake freely of the Tree of Life as long as they did not eat of the Tree of Knowledge of Good and Evil. But once they ate of the forbidden tree, they were cut off from the Tree of Life.

So, in the midst of the garden we have these two trees. And we have a Man and a Woman living in the garden, in fellowship with the triune God who created them. We don't know how long they wandered among these two trees. But one fateful day something happened.

The Serpent

> Now the serpent was more crafty than any beast of the field which the LORD God had made. (Gen 3:1a)

---

1. The text implies that these two trees pre-existed the Garden. They did not grow out of the ground in the same manner as all of the other trees.

2. My understanding of these two trees is rooted in teaching on the subject from Fatherheart Ministries. There is more to the subject than I have been able to cover in this chapter. For a deeper understanding, I highly recommend the book *The Ancient Road Rediscovered* by M. James Jordan.

The serpent here was not a snake on the ground as we may imagine when we hear the word serpent.[3] The Hebrew word *nachash*, which is translated here as serpent, is derived from a very similar word (also transliterated as *nachash*) which means to enchant or to learn by experience. This serpent was an intelligent being, appearing to be wiser and more persuasive than any beast of the field. Ezekiel describes him in this manner:

> You were the seal of perfection, full of wisdom and perfect in beauty. You were in Eden, the garden of God; every precious stone adorned you: carnelian, chrysolite and emerald, topaz, onyx and jasper, lapis lazuli, turquoise and beryl. Your settings and mountings were made of gold; on the day you were created they were prepared. You were anointed as a guardian cherub, for so I ordained you. You were on the holy mount of God; you walked among the fiery stones. You were blameless in your ways from the day you were created till wickedness was found in you. Through your widespread trade you were filled with violence, and you sinned. So I drove you in disgrace from the mount of God, and I expelled you, guardian cherub, from among the fiery stones. Your heart became proud on account of your beauty, and you corrupted your wisdom because of your splendor. So I threw you to the earth; I made a spectacle of you before kings. (Ezek 28:12b–17)

This creature, perfect in beauty, was a guardian cherub in the garden of Eden. It is possible that his purpose as a guardian cherub in the garden was to prevent the Man and the Woman from eating of the Tree of Knowledge of Good and Evil. Or perhaps he was that tree. In any case, his wisdom became corrupted, and he persuaded the Woman and the Man to consume that corrupted wisdom.

The Knowledge of Good and Evil

The problem with the knowledge of good and evil is not just the knowledge of evil. The knowledge of good is also a problem, because the root issue is neither good nor evil in itself, but the whole spectrum of good and evil.

The knowledge of good and evil rests on differentiating that which is good from that which is evil. Everything comes into a scale of comparison.

---

3. His appearance did not become like that until later (verse 14) when he was cursed to crawl on his belly and eat dust.

Doing good things would seemingly increase my value, while doing evil things would have the opposite effect.

Mankind was not created to discern between good and evil. We were created to relate to Father God in love. The one who loves does not need to be told to do good or to avoid evil, because love leads us to choose that which is pleasing and desirable in the eyes of the one whom we love. But the knowledge of good and evil blinds us to the ways of love and instead opens our eyes to a corrupted wisdom of judgment.

In this corrupted wisdom, good becomes a mechanism for gaining acceptance. And those who do not appear to be good enough come under condemnation. Typically, we end up expending great effort to hide our shortcomings behind fig leaves in order to not seem to be naked (as it were). And we tend to condemn those whom we deem to be less good than they should be. This is not a life of peace.

The Tree of Life

The Tree of Life is completely different.

The apostle Peter referred to Jesus as the author or originator of life. Jesus said that he came so that we would have life in abundance. Proverbs states that Wisdom is a tree of life.[4] It is therefore natural to conclude (as early church fathers such as Bonaventure and Augustine have done) that the Tree of Life is Jesus.

God is love. And Jesus, the Son of God, is a complete and perfect image of—the exact representation of—the nature of God. It follows, therefore, that the Tree of Life is all about love.

In the framework of love there is no comparison. There is no scale of acceptability. There is no measure of good or bad. Love chooses to accept unconditionally. It has been said that love is blind. And that is certainly true in the sense that love does not look to the knowledge of good and evil.

When the Man ate the fruit of the Tree of Knowledge of Good and Evil, their eyes were opened.[5] In other words the Man and Woman became able to see something which they had previously not seen: Evil. Until then, they had only been able to see good. Evil was present in the Garden, at least in the form of the serpent, but perhaps also in their own potential for evil.

---

4. See Acts 3:15, John 10:10, and Prov 3:18. See also the description of Wisdom in Proverbs 8, which portrays the originator of life, Jesus the Messiah.

5. See Gen 3:7

And yet, as long as they could only perceive good they were enveloped in love. Love renders evil powerless.[6]

The Law and the Prophets

After having eaten from the forbidden tree, the Man and Woman were banished from the garden in order to prevent them from eating of the Tree of Life while they were enslaved to the knowledge of good and evil.

Much of the remainder of the Old Testament is a history of how the knowledge of good and evil leads people to destroy one another. It also encompasses the Law and the Prophets: the Word of God to a people consumed by the corrupted wisdom of the knowledge of good and evil.

The Law makes sense in a good and evil framework. The Law is all about doing things in order to be accepted, as well as about the consequences of not doing the good which the Law requires. The Prophets also communicated largely in a framework of good and evil: their message is mostly framed in terms of rewards and punishments. But the Law and Prophets are not the final word of God.[7]

Jesus said that he came to fulfill the Law and Prophets and that they were proclaimed until John the Baptist; after which the good news of the Kingdom of God has been released.[8] Jesus is referring to The Great Shift. The work that he came to accomplish made it possible for humans to walk away from the framework of good and evil, and once again eat of the Tree of Life. He made this very clear when he summarized the entirety of the Law and Prophets into a single word: Love.[9]

Now, you might be thinking: Hold on here. Jesus may have fulfilled the Law, but he did not abolish it. That is a valid point. And it may lead you to conclude that you must continue to perform all of the ordinances and rituals prescribed by the Law of Moses. But I don't think so.

The word in Matt 5:17 which is translated as *fulfill*, means to fill completely full so that there is nothing lacking. It implies completion, fullness, and consummation. If Jesus has fulfilled the Law then our own performance

---

6. See Col 2:15

7. See Heb 1:1–2. See also Heb 7:18–19 and Gal 3:10–29. Note that, in Gal 3:21, the Law can not impart life.

8. See Matt 5:17–19 and Luke 16:16

9. See Matt 22:37–40

of the requirements of the Law can contribute nothing. Which means that nothing is gained by our obedience.

Don't get me wrong here. I am not saying that the Law of Moses has no value. Neither am I saying that we are to disregard the commands of our Lord. But our keeping of the Law has no value, because it has been fulfilled in Jesus.

Servant or Friend?

In the parable of the prodigal son, there is an interesting insight. After the son had lost everything and then came to his senses, he said to himself that he would return home and ask to be a servant in the house of his father. He reasoned that being a servant of his father was actually a pretty good life.

The Law of Moses was given to a people who, at the time of their deliverance, knew only a life of servant-hood. Moses, the Servant of God,[10] delivered prescriptions for behavior to a people who were accustomed to being told what to do. And the Law of Moses is a good thing—within a knowledge of good and evil framework.

The prodigal son saw the benefits of being a servant in the house of his father and (because of his shame and guilt) he would have been satisfied to live in that kind of servant-hood. But servant-hood is far less than what we are created for. And if we find ourselves satisfied living as a servant of our Very Good God, it can actually prevent us from living as a son or daughter of our Very Good Father.

The people who Moses led out of Egypt were descendants of Abraham, the friend of God.[11] Abraham was a man of faith, a man who lived his life in a way that pleased God. Abraham and the Lord God developed a friendship without any law. Because friendship is built through relationship and not through keeping commandments.

The fulfillment of the Law, through The Great Shift, has opened wide the door to friendship with God rather than servant-hood to God.

---

10. See 1 Chr 6:49, 2 Chr 24:9, Neh 10:29, Dan 9:11
11. See 2 Chr 20:7, Isa 41:8, Jas 2:23

Eating

When the man and woman were banished from the garden, the main reason for their expulsion was that "he must not be allowed to reach out his hand and take also from the Tree of Life and eat, and live forever."[12]

You may look at this and think that since Adam had been commanded not to eat from the forbidden tree lest he die then this banishment was a punishment for their disobedience. They must die and therefore must be denied access to the Tree of Life.

Or you might see the grace in this banishment: that by being denied access to the Tree of Life, they would be protected from having to spend eternity under the curse of the knowledge of good and evil.

Although both of these perspectives bear some degree of truth, there is yet more to be gleaned from this reason. Did you notice the word *also*? Having eaten of the Tree of Knowledge of Good and Evil, he must not *also* eat of the Tree of Life. In order to eat of the Tree of Life, it would first be necessary to make an end of the knowledge of good and evil.

Even though the Law of Moses is an expression of the knowledge of good and evil, it also points toward something better. Have you noticed that, to a great degree, the worship prescribed by the Law is related to food and fellowship? There were clear instructions about which foods were clean and unclean. And for the most part, after an animal was sacrificed, the meat would be eaten by the worshipers. Perhaps the clearest example of this is the instruction for how to spend the tithe.[13] Worship was to be a party, a feast together with God. In this setting, love, peace, joy and fellowship were the focus.

When Jesus died on the Cross, several things happened:

- The curtain in the temple, which symbolized the wall of separation between God and mankind, was torn in two from top to bottom. This curtain was decorated with cherubim—the same beings that were set to guard the way to the Tree of Life.

- Many dead people were raised to life. There was a release of unprecedented resurrection power. Life broke forth.

---

12. Gen 3:22b
13. See Deut 14:22–29

- The certificate of debt that was against us was nailed to the cross. Rulers and authorities were disarmed.[14] The curse of the knowledge of good and evil lost its power to enslave.
- The Tree of Life was made freely available for us to eat of its fruit. Everlasting life became available to the sons and daughters of God.

You might wonder about that last point. So let's take a look at what Jesus has to say about eating:

> "Very truly I tell you, the one who believes has eternal life. I am the bread of life. Your ancestors ate the manna in the wilderness, yet they died. But here is the bread that comes down from heaven, which anyone may eat and not die. I am the living bread that came down from heaven. Whoever eats this bread will live forever. This bread is my flesh, which I will give for the life of the world." Then the Jews began to argue sharply among themselves, "How can this man give us his flesh to eat?" Jesus said to them, "Very truly I tell you, unless you eat the flesh of the Son of Man and drink his blood, you have no life in you. Whoever eats my flesh and drinks my blood has eternal life, and I will raise them up at the last day. For my flesh is real food and my blood is real drink. Whoever eats my flesh and drinks my blood remains in me, and I in them. Just as the living Father sent me and I live because of the Father, so the one who feeds on me will live because of me. This is the bread that came down from heaven. Your ancestors ate manna and died, but whoever feeds on this bread will live forever." (John 6:47–58)

This is a complex passage, where Jesus is speaking with an imagery that seems a bit shocking. For example, he refers to his flesh as real food and his blood as real drink. Taking that literally is, to say the least, a bit macabre. But if we look at real food in light of what Jesus said to his disciples after meeting the woman at the well, it makes a bit more sense. He said, "My food, is to do the will of him who sent me and to finish his work."[15] He also spoke of his flesh as living bread, which on another occasion he described as being like "every word that comes from the mouth of God."[16]

Jesus summed up this passage by proclaiming: "Whoever feeds on this bread will live forever." Even his disciples were offended by this claim. But, to make things as clear as possible, Jesus said that his words were full of

---

14. See Col 2:15
15. John 4:34
16. Matt 4:4

Spirit and life.[17] So what does it mean to live forever? Jesus said that eternal life is to know the only true God, and Jesus Christ, whom God has sent.[18] So, to feed on this bread is to know our God, to be filled with the ways of his heart.

Putting all of these things together makes it clear that Jesus, the Word of God, the Word made flesh, is the Tree of Life. To know and experience (that is, to feed on, to consume, and to internalize) the nature and person and life of Jesus is to eat of that tree. And as that life flows into our being we become filled with eternal life.

The Law of Liberty

OK, that was pretty heady stuff. What does it mean in practice? Simply put, we are once again invited to eat the fruit of the Tree of Life. And consequently, we need no longer eat the fruit of the knowledge of good and evil. Or, to put it another way, we are no longer under the law of Moses, but rather invited to speak and act in accordance with the law of liberty, the law of the Spirit—the law of love.[19]

The law of Moses is full of the knowledge of good and evil. Or, as Paul said, "I would not have known what sin was had it not been for the law."[20] Anything that we do or think or say, if it is based on discerning between good and evil, comes from eating of that tree. Whether it be our own feelings of inadequacy or condemnation, or the judgments we make about others, it is all wrong tree thinking. When our actions are motivated by following (or breaking) the rules, then we are eating the fruit of the Tree of Knowledge of Good and Evil.

The law of liberty is completely different. It is entirely and completely based on love. And love keeps no account of wrongs.[21] In the realm of true love, there is no good or evil, there is only love and acceptance. As we eat the fruit of this tree of love, the love of God is poured out in our hearts, leading our desires and longings to become more and more in line with the nature of our Father. Just as David sang: "Take delight in the LORD, and

17. John 6:63
18. John 17:3
19. See Jas 1:25, 2:12, John 15:7, and Rom 8:1–2
20. Rom 7:7
21. 1 Cor 13:5

he will give you the desires of your heart."[22] His law of liberty is written in our hearts. We no longer need to focus on doing what is right, because it becomes our nature to walk in the ways that are dear to our beloved's heart.

Perhaps this sounds too good to be true. Or maybe you are thinking, "That can't be right." Can we really just live our lives doing whatever we feel like doing? Well, yes! And no!

The problem here is that our way of thinking is so immersed in the knowledge of good and evil that we have trouble wrapping our minds around this law of liberty. When we see someone walking in freedom, something inside of us wants to say, "But what if they do that which is wrong? What if they break the rules?"

In one sense, the law of liberty means that it doesn't matter if we do what is good or what is evil. And those who eat the fruit of the Tree of Knowledge of Good and Evil will struggle with that concept. How can there be no rules? Can we really live without knowing what is right or wrong?

The fruit of the Tree of Life helps us gain a different perspective. Jesus said that the Law could be summed up in two simple commands: Love the Lord with all your heart, soul, and mind; and love everyone else as well.[23] In his letter, James describes the law of liberty in the context of faith being demonstrated through the presence of good works. The one who truly loves will prioritize the interests of their beloved.[24] For the one who loves, it becomes natural to do what is good without having to follow rules. It is no longer necessary to choose good rather than evil, because choosing to love always looks for the best.

Under the law of liberty we are free to do as we desire, because the love which Father God has poured into our hearts leads us to desire to bring him pleasure. Under the law of liberty we are neither condemned nor punished for breaking the rules. Under the law of liberty, sins are not bad because they are sinful, so much as they are bad because they destroy us. The law of the Spirit has set us free from the law of sin and death,[25] but the consequences of sin still remain. Breaking the speed limit will not send you to hell, but it could still lead to a speeding ticket or a tragic traffic accident. Most of the commandments in the Law are there because Father

---

22. Ps 37:4
23. See Matt 22:36–40
24. See John 14:23
25. Rom 8:2

God knows that those things lead to pain, sorrow, and destruction rather than to peace, love, and joy.

When Jesus invited people to join his company, he said: "Follow me." He did not actually call people to *obey* him, but to *follow* him. Although Jesus occasionally spoke of obeying his commandments, his commandments were always wrapped in a context of love.[26] The point here is that our Lord is really not looking for servants who will obey his will. Rather, he is looking for followers who will walk in his ways and relate to him in love. He is looking for a people who will be children to the Father and a bride to the Son.

In a healthy marriage, the wife is not the servant of the husband. In fact, we would tend to look upon a man as having psychopathic tendencies, if he demands that his wife constantly obey his commands and submit to his will. Looking at our relationship to our Lord through the knowledge of good and evil leads us to relate to him primarily through obedience and submission. That is *not* the kind of relationship Father God is looking for. Those who eat of the Tree of Life are not under the control of obedience to commands. Rather they become followers through love.

I experienced an example of how this works (without actually realizing it at the time) years before I began to really understand this law of liberty. When I was in my twenties, I worked as an engineer at a university research institute. About mid-way through my time there, the institute chose a new director: a Japanese man who had been at that institute for most of his career. Although he was a renowned researcher, he was also a soft-spoken man. Not long after he became director, I began to understand that when he happened to casually make a suggestion about something, his words carried the weight of a command. He never actually commanded, and I never knew him to punish or disrespect anyone for not doing as he suggested. But it was simply unnatural to not fulfill his requests. There was something about the greatness that he carried, mixed with the respect and honor that he showed to his colleagues (regardless of how much we may have deserved it) that led us to freely do his bidding.

A meeting with true greatness is usually accompanied by an element of fear. But fear can play out in two very different ways, depending on how we perceive that greatness. If we view a great person as powerful, demanding, and judgmental then we will probably fear their wrath. If, however, we perceive greatness wrapped in love and honor then we would more likely

---

26. For example, see John 14:21–24 and 15:9–17

respond with awe, respect, and a joy in meeting and being touched by their greatness. This is what the fear of the Lord actually looks like.

Now, our God is much greater and far more loving than any of the great people I have met (or heard about). So it should be much easier for us to submit to his love and naturally live out his desires. His Spirit is constantly whispering to us with gentle expressions of his ways.

> The mind governed by the flesh is death, but the mind governed by the Spirit is life and peace. (Rom 8:6)

Walking in the law of liberty is a life of peace. With our eyes fixed firmly on the author and finisher of our faith, our every step will be a step into closer alignment with his heart. Nothing can shake us from the firm foundation of his love. No one can accuse us of not being good enough.

What You See Is What You Get

It may be that you feel like this description of the law of liberty sounds a lot like "hyper-grace." Hyper-grace is a term which has become popular in recent years to describe teaching which leans more toward the love of God and away from the holiness of God. To a certain extent, warnings about some expressions of grace-focused church life may be justified, because there do exist congregations where sinful behavior appears to be rampant; and that can be very damaging. And yet, much of the critical warnings about hyper-grace seem to be formulated from a knowledge of good and evil perspective.

In his letter to the Galatians, Paul wrote about a gospel which is no gospel. That letter was, in fact, written as a response to the hyper-grace accusers of his own time. These were the people whom Paul claimed "had infiltrated our ranks to spy on the freedom we have in Christ Jesus and to make us slaves."[27] They were people who, with backing of the scriptures, tried to impose a gospel different from the law of liberty.

As previously stated, under the law of liberty we can do whatever we wish. But only within the framework of love. As long as we are feeding on the Tree of Life and seeking to know the heart of Father God and walk in his ways, we are free to do whatever we wish—because we walk in love.

---

27. Gal 2:4. Trevor Galpin has written an excellent description of the relationship between the two trees of Genesis and the two gospels of Galatians in his book *The Story of Paul: The Early Years*.

Perhaps it all boils down to this question: What is the fundamental characteristic of the nature of God? There are many words that can be used to describe the nature of God. He is almighty, omniscient, glorious, and so forth. But most of his characteristics are expressions of his core nature. How we see the core nature of God depends on our perspective.

> Then the eyes of both of them were opened, and they realized they were naked (Gen 3:7a)

When Adam ate the fruit of the Tree of Knowledge of Good and Evil his perspective changed immediately. The text states that "their eyes were opened," which at first glance might lead us to think that their perspective previously had been limited. But the phrase rather implies that they became able to see something which previously had been hidden from sight.

This change of perspective led them to feel something they never before had experienced: They felt naked. I believe that this feeling of nakedness went far deeper than just the fact that their bodies were not covered, because in verse 10 we see that this feeling of nakedness was accompanied by another new experience: Fear. Never before had they experienced fear in the presence of God, but now they were acutely aware that they wanted something that could cover up that which had become visible to them.

In other words, eating from the Tree of Knowledge of Good and Evil allowed them to see more, but they no longer saw accurately. It was, and remains, a tragic change of perspective.

Our perspective does not define the true nature of God. But it does shape what we experience him to be like. And we can easily live under the deception that our experience depicts the truth.

Holiness

Those who see God through the lens of the knowledge of good and evil will likely conclude that, at the core, God is holy, and that everything else about him is framed and influenced by his holiness. The Law and the Prophets build a very good case for this perspective.

With holiness at the core, all of God's dealings with mankind will operate in the light of good and evil. His wrath, his requirements, our value, our acceptability; are all seen with eyes that have been opened to the knowledge of good and evil. So God appears to be angry with us, making us fearful and leading us to feel inadequate (naked).

When God says something like: "Remember to set apart a day of rest each week,"[28] the knowledge of good and evil leads us to hear: "If you do anything that could appear to be work on the holy day of rest, then I will punish you for failing to meet my requirements."

The fruit of the Tree of Knowledge of Good and Evil presents to us a God who appears to be a strict and demanding taskmaster. This is what God looks like when we eat from that tree.

Love

However, looking from the perspective of the Tree of Life helps us to see that, at the core, God is love. Everything else about him, including his holiness, is framed by love. The fruit of the Tree of Life portrays a God who is a Good Father.

A Tree of Life perspective does not make God any less holy. Rather, it enhances our experience of his holiness. Instead of feeling fear when we meet this holy God, we see his holiness as a thing of awesome beauty. We meet the call to "worship the Lord in the beauty of holiness"[29] with the thrill of love and acceptance in an atmosphere of incredible and overwhelming beauty.

It is the love of God that brought about the redemptive work of the Cross. The love of God reached through holiness to do a work of incomprehensible depth and wonder. Were the core nature of God his holiness, then he could have continued to be God without devising a salvation for mankind. But he would not be the God of love without the atonement of the Cross.[30]

The penalty for all sin has been paid. But that does not mean that we are free to sin. Because sin is, by definition, missing the mark.[31] The law of liberty sets us free to walk in love, to draw near to the God of love, to learn his heart and to choose to walk in his ways. In fact, it is not possible to sin when fully walking in love.

The problem of so-called hyper-grace is not the grace. It is our failure to connect with the Tree of Life. But any reaction to hyper-grace which tries to correct its failure through a regime of legalism, is bound to the knowledge of good and evil. There is no peace there.

28. Exod 20:8
29. See KJV 1 Chr 16:29, 2 Chr 20:21, and Psa 27:2 and 96:9
30. See 1 John 4:7–19
31. More on that in a few pages.

The Heart of the Child

Yeast

One day, while out on a boat ride, Jesus had a somewhat odd dialog with his disciples. Here's how Matthew, who was in the boat at the time, recorded it in his gospel:

> When they went across the lake, the disciples forgot to take bread. "Be careful," Jesus said to them. "Be on your guard against the yeast of the Pharisees and Sadducees." They discussed this among themselves and said, "It is because we didn't bring any bread." Aware of their discussion, Jesus asked, "You of little faith, why are you talking among yourselves about having no bread? Do you still not understand? Don't you remember the five loaves for the five thousand, and how many basketfuls you gathered? Or the seven loaves for the four thousand, and how many basketfuls you gathered? How is it you don't understand that I was not talking to you about bread? But be on your guard against the yeast of the Pharisees and Sadducees." Then they understood that he was not telling them to guard against the yeast used in bread, but against the teaching of the Pharisees and Sadducees. (Matt 16:5–12)

Perhaps the disciples were getting used to these situations where they really had no clue what Jesus was talking about. But it was undoubtedly a little embarrassing for them. You can almost imagine them sitting there in the boat with puzzled looks on their faces, whispering to one another something like: "What have we done wrong now? Hey, John, you didn't forget to bring the lunch boxes, did you?"

I guess that the disciples didn't recall just then that, sometime earlier, Jesus had told them that the kingdom of heaven is like yeast mixed into a large batch of bread dough.[32] That was another case where Jesus wasn't talking about the bread that you bake, but rather about the real food from the Tree of Life. The deal about yeast is that it is a small and seemingly insignificant ingredient which has a huge influence on the result.

Parents seldom teach their children the things of life (attitudes, values, behavior, etc) in a classroom or lecture setting. For the most part, these things are learned through interaction between parent and child. And, in a healthy family situation, much of that interaction takes place around the table at meal times.

Conversation around the table can touch on pretty much any subject. And, like yeast, the values and behaviors of the parents are transferred to

---

32. See Matt 13:33

the children through that interaction, greatly influencing who the children become.

Yeast in this context is the beliefs, attitudes, and values that we allow to shape and form our thinking and behavior. The yeast of the Pharisees was a system of rules that controlled outward behavior but did not shape the values of the heart to match that behavior.

In Jesus' day, the Pharisees were enforcing about three times as many rules as were found in the Law of Moses. The Law was given within a knowledge of good and evil framework, and the corrupted wisdom of that framework led to a Pharisaical system which was fully corrupt.

Let's take honesty as an example. In the simplicity of the ten commandments, we are instructed to speak honestly (to not bear false witness). But in the Pharisaical system, rules were devised to define when it would be acceptable to lie to and defraud your neighbor.[33] Eating from the corrupted wisdom of the Tree of Knowledge of Good and Evil produces this kind of yeast.

Which is perhaps why there is a focus in the Law on differentiating between clean and unclean foods. Not so much because of the foods themselves, but because unclean "real food" is so destructive. When Jesus said to guard yourself against the yeast of the Pharisees, he was in essence saying: "Let no unclean food pass your lips." He was saying to watch over your heart, out of which flow the springs of life.[34]

Sins vs. Sin

The knowledge of good and evil leads to a focus on sins. Questions like "Is it a sin to do . . . ?" or "How can I keep myself from falling into the sin of . . . ?" are birthed in the knowledge of good and evil. Although every sinful act has its destructive consequences, Father God is really not so very focused on all of these sins.

The larger problem is Sin, which is perhaps best defined as "We all, like sheep, have gone astray, each of us has turned to our own way."[35] Sin is doing things your own way. The sinful acts that we do, or have done, are merely symptoms of Sin. And Sin is the business of controlling and directing our own lives, rather than eating from the Tree of Life.

---

33. See Matt 23:16–22
34. Prov 4:23 NASB
35. Isa 53:6

The Heart of the Child

> God is opposed to the proud, but gives grace to the humble. Therefore humble yourselves under the mighty hand of God, that He may exalt you at the proper time, casting all your anxiety on Him, because He cares for you. (1 Pet 5:5b–7 NASB)

In these verses, the key word is *casting*. Peter defines humility as turning over control of your life to God—especially the things you worry about and the things you feel you need to have taken care of. Pride, which is another word for Sin, is living in the illusion that you are in control of your own life. It is the opposite of trust and the opposite of faith.

Jesus, on the other hand, lived a life on this earth without Sin. The key to a sinless life, in his own words, is: "Very truly I tell you, the Son can do nothing by himself; he can do only what he sees his Father doing, because whatever the Father does the Son also does."[36] That, in a nutshell, is the opposite of Sin.

A focus on sins rather than Sin leads us also into the realm of accusation. We might have a tendency to try to downplay our own sins by accusing others. This is what God was saying to Cain before he killed his brother Abel. "If you do what is right, will you not be accepted? But if you do not do what is right, sin is crouching at your door; it desires to have you, but you must rule over it."[37] Cain made a choice not to listen to the Author of Life, but rather look upon (accuse) his brother as the source of his problems. The sin of murder was merely a symptom of Sin, when Cain chose to turn to his own way.

This perspective of Sin is a challenge for Norwegians and perhaps even more so for Americans, because both cultures value independence and self-sufficiency highly. In fact, the United States was founded through a Declaration of Independence, and that independent spirit permeates the culture to this day. However, in the culture of the Kingdom of Heaven, independence is not a good thing. In the eyes of God, a unilateral declaration of independence is actually an act of rebellion—the root of Sin. To live in this way is to choose the Tree of Knowledge of Good and Evil, and reject the Tree of Life.

---

36. John 5: 19. See also John 5:30, 8:28, and 12:49
37. Gen 4:7

The Two Books

Perhaps you may be wondering how the final judgment fits into all of this. If there is no longer to be any knowledge of good and evil, then what about the judgment at the end of the age? Let's take a look at it:

> Then I saw a great white throne and him who was seated on it. The earth and the heavens fled from his presence, and there was no place for them. And I saw the dead, great and small, standing before the throne, and books were opened. Another book was opened, which is the book of life. The dead were judged according to what they had done as recorded in the books. The sea gave up the dead that were in it, and death and Hades gave up the dead that were in them, and each person was judged according to what they had done. Then death and Hades were thrown into the lake of fire. The lake of fire is the second death. Anyone whose name was not found written in the book of life was thrown into the lake of fire. (Rev 20:11–15)

The books here correlate to the two trees. There are books, in which are recorded the deeds of every person who has ever lived. At the end of the age, everyone will be judged according their deeds as recorded in those books. Everyone will be judged according to the knowledge of good and evil.

That is, everyone *except* those whose names are written in the Book of Life. The Book of Life, like the Tree of Life, has no knowledge of right and wrong. Rather, it is simply a list of those who are beloved!

The death and resurrection of Jesus has brought about forgiveness of sin. And true forgiveness means that there is no record of wrongs. So, at the judgment, those who eat of the Tree of Life—those who feed on the true bread that came down from heaven—will find that there is no record of their lives in the books, except that their name will be found in the Book of Life.

4

A Culture of Freedom

AFTER A SHORT INTRODUCTION, the book of Revelation begins with seven specific messages from Jesus to seven churches. In the last of these messages, Jesus says:

> Those whom I love I rebuke and discipline. So be earnest and repent. Here I am! I stand at the door and knock. If anyone hears my voice and opens the door, I will come in and eat with that person, and they with me. (Rev 3:19–20)

The context here is a people whose love has grown cold. Jesus expresses, rather sternly, his dissatisfaction with their lukewarm state and their lack of insight into just how far off course they have gotten.

From a knowledge of good and evil perspective, we might look at this situation and see an angry God who would drive these lukewarm people away and punish them for their unfaithfulness. But from a Tree of Life perspective, the situation looks quite different. After somewhat harshly exposing their true state, Jesus says that he loves them and desires to eat and fellowship with them.

When Jesus speaks words of correction or rebuke, he does not speak as an accuser. Accusation is the language of the devil.[1] Jesus only speaks what he hears his Father saying. He never speaks as the enemy would speak. Though words of correction may be uncomfortable, the words of Jesus are spoken to bring peace, restoration, and wholeness.

---

1. See Rev 12:9–10

When Jesus stands at the door and knocks, it is not something to fear. Perfect love drives out fear, because fear has to do with punishment.[2] When Jesus comes to eat with us, he comes in perfect love. And in perfect love there is neither fear nor punishment.

The rebuke of Jesus is never meant to bring fear or punishment, because whatever it may be which Jesus would rebuke or correct, it has already been forgiven through his death on the Cross. There is nothing to punish. There is no punishment to fear. There is only a meal to be shared.

When dining with Jesus, the knowledge of good and evil is not on the menu. Instead, the fruit of the Tree of Life is served. This banquet table is a place of peace, because we are forgiven. The books of right and wrong have been set aside. Forgiveness opens the door to life.

Potential

One of the things which I find fascinating is how Father God looks at failure. I've seen it many times, in my own life and in the lives of others. It is also clear to see in the stories of bible hero murderers, such as Moses, David and Paul.

Paul wrote that Gods gifts and his call are irrevocable.[3] In other words, when Father God gives gifts, they are truly given. It is not a gift if it is based on our achievements. It is not truly a gift if it can be retracted.

Think about that. When God (who knows the end from the beginning) opens doors for us to walk into our call, he does so completely aware of our failings along the way. Despite that, he calls and he gives gifts.

His gifts and his call are given toward our potential, not for our performance. He has planted in each of us great potential and an awesome birthright. And it is his delight to see that potential develop and blossom.

Most important of all: He is not in any way afraid of us falling or failing along the way. I have great joy in watching my young granddaughter fumble her way into new and exciting discoveries in her life. And Father God is a far better father than I can claim to be.

So, whether it be a fumble or a stumble or outright rebellion, God does not reclaim or regret his gifts or his call.

If there is one area we tend to find this particularly challenging, it is when church leaders fall. I have known a few church leaders who have

2. 1 John 4:18
3. Rom 11:29

shown great potential, walked in favor and giftings, and had a clear calling on their lives. But they (just like all of us) also have weaknesses in their lives. And eventually some failure or fall has come to light and they have been stripped of their ministry.

When that happens, not only the world but also we in the church can be quick to condemn. We tend to treat them as lepers—unforgivable, cursed by God, never again to be trusted. We wouldn't want to be seen associating with them, perhaps out of some misguided fear that their failure might rub off on us.

OK. Maybe it's not always quite as bad as that. But I have seen it happen. And I have seen the pain in former leaders who feel ostracized, unforgiven, and basically finished. Over and out. Done for. However much they may have preached forgiveness, their hearers have none for them.

And yet . . .

> If you, God, kept record on wrongdoings, who would stand a chance? As it turns out, forgiveness is your habit, and that's why you're worshiped. (Ps 130:3-4 The Message)

Love keeps no record of wrongs. And God is love! It is his habit to forgive. There is no failure too big to be forgiven. There is no height from which we can fall that is too large for recovery.

Forgiveness Should Be Contagious

Forgiveness is a big deal in the Kingdom of Heaven. It is so central to the culture of the Kingdom that no one may enter there without having experienced forgiveness. And no one will thrive there unless they learn to become a forgiver.

Peace is quenched when forgiveness is withheld. Holding on to an offense rather than releasing it through forgiveness is like trying to put out a fire by dousing it in gasoline. The consequences can be dire, and it is usually the person who withholds forgiveness that ends up getting burned.

Jesus was very clear about the consequences of withholding forgiveness.[4] But perhaps his clearest illustration is in the parable of the unforgiving servant.[5] That parable tells the story of a man with a debt so large that it could never be repaid. Beyond all hope, the debt is forgiven. But when

---

4. See Matt 6:14-15, Mark 11:25, and Luke 6:37
5. Matt 18:23-35

this man then comes upon a friend whose debt to him remains unpaid, rather than responding with forgiveness in the manner of that which he had received, he turns his friend over to punishment. His failure to forgive results in he himself being tortured. And then Jesus says that his Father will do likewise to anyone who fails to forgive.

Once again, if you look at this from a knowledge of good and evil perspective, then you might end up seeing God as a hard taskmaster. But the truth is that we were not created to carry offenses. Holding on to an offense causes hardness and bitterness to grow in a way that eats up the soul of the unforgiving person. These are the torturers. There is no peace there.

The fruit of the Tree of Life leads us to forgive. In an atmosphere of love, no offense remains. In order to truly eat of the Tree of Life, we must unlearn the knowledge of good and evil.

Communicating Freedom

To forgive is to set the offender free from the punishment that is due them. But forgiving from the heart also sets the offended person free from the torture of their own pain and bitterness. This is essential for peacemaking.

Forgiveness is not pretending like the offense never happened. Neither is forgiveness acting as if it was OK after all. It was *not* OK; there *was* an offense and losses were suffered. Those things may take time to heal, but they should not stand in the way of communicating freedom.

Forgiveness is saying: "I cancel the debt." It is setting the offender free from the requirement of repayment, restitution or punishment for the pain that was inflicted or the loss that was incurred. Or, more correctly, it is relinquishing the right to require recompense, and turning it over to the only person with sufficient wisdom to handle the case in a manner worthy of the culture of the Kingdom: Papa God.

Forgiveness is not merely an emotional thing, even though we may go through a lot of emotions in the process. Forgiveness is a heart issue, where the love of God which is poured out in our hearts leads us to proclaim freedom in the face of the accuser. It may take an act of the will for you to choose to develop a forgiving heart; but when the decision is taken there, the practice of forgiving from the heart will grow in fruitful soil. It may be that you need to remind yourself of your act of forgiving multiple times in order to establish the decision in your mind and emotions, but the deeper the roots of forgiveness grow in your heart, the easier this will become.

The Heart of the Child

A friend of mine told me about how, in processing forgiveness for a major offense in her life, God had led her to calculate the total cost of the offense. She estimated the compensation that might be awarded to her by a court of law. And then she imagined herself ripping the payment to shreds. This helped her to move forgiveness from her head to her heart, and gave her a reference point for experiencing freedom from the pain of the offense.

One of the most common emotions we need to deal with when we have been hurt or offended is anger. Unresolved anger gives the devil a foothold.[6] A foothold is a place that gives an opportunity to stay attached. In other words, if we don't deal with our anger, then we allow demonic power to establish a foundation in our life where it has a place to stand. Forgiveness is like a sledgehammer that smashes the foothold and causes the devil to lose his grip. Forgiveness may seem unfair or impractical, but it releases freedom by pulling up the source of anger at its root.

The enemy of our souls, the devil, is also called the accuser of our brothers and sisters.[7] Often in a situation calling for forgiveness, the voice of the accuser is there demanding a righteousness in the form of punishment. You may not actually hear a voice in your head (most people don't). But have you considered that, when facing a decision to forgive, you tend to meet a barrage of thoughts about what the person has done, how offended or hurt you are, and so on? That is the accuser at work.

The jailers and torturers in the final scene of the parable of the unforgiving servant represent the accuser. Because the barrage of accusations flooding your mind will continue, if you do not forgive. This barrage has several goals (none of which lead to peace), including: To keep the wound open and festering, to get you to agree with the accusations, and occasionally also to remind you how inadequate you are for having not forgiven. Not much freedom in that. And as long as you are in agreement with these accusations, they will have a controlling influence in your life.

So perhaps even more than setting the offender free, forgiveness brings freedom to the person offended. And it opens the door to healing, by cleansing and closing the wound that the accusations have infected.

---

6. See Eph 4:27
7. See Rev 12:10

A Culture of Freedom

Forgiveness Hits Close to Home

Just a few days after I started writing this chapter, I received word of a major act of betrayal; an issue which is large in many dimensions and affects me greatly. That led me to put writing on hold for a few weeks. After all, what authority do I have to write about forgiveness when I've got an unresolved offense hanging around?

Forgiveness is a fairly easy concept to face when the offenses are not very significant or the cost seems to not be so big. But when the betrayal feels large or the loss seems irreparable, then it becomes costly to look forgiveness in the face.

Even though I very much want to forgive, at least in principle, I am faced with a wide range of emotions and questions. Could I have misunderstood? Might it be possible to negotiate? Was I so wrong in trusting that person? What is this doing to my relationships? What am I going to do with my pain? Choosing to forgive does not necessarily sort all of these things out—at least not in a hurry. But they must be worked through.

Forgiving can feel a lot like losing. But, as we saw in chapter 2, to lose is to win. Forgiveness releases peace and freedom. It is at the core of The Great Shift. And often (but not always) it can open the door to restoring broken relationships.

The Road to Peace

The road to peace frequently passes through the valley of forgiveness. Therefore, a peacemaker needs not only to be quick to forgive, but also adept at defusing conflict and releasing freedom.

The road through the valley of forgiveness passes by several milestones, many of which deserve our attention. You may not always need to stop at all of them, but in most cases it will be helpful to do so. Some of these stops may feel like an oasis of refreshment, while others may feel more like an engine breakdown.

- Invite Jesus into the details. Work through the facts with him. Share your feelings and thoughts with him. Ask him how he sees it. You might imagine yourself eating a meal together with him while you discuss these things.

- Make a decision to forgive. Declare that the offender is free from punishment, that the debt is canceled. Whether you declare these things before Papa God in your own heart, or also speak them to the offender may be a difficult decision. The purpose of forgiveness is freedom, so that should be a guiding principle in choosing the specifics of how to communicate forgiveness. If the offender is unlikely to understand or acknowledge the offense, then often speaking forgiveness to the offender will more likely lead to misunderstanding, anger, or confusion than lead to freedom.

- Forgive from the heart. Turn your heart toward forgiveness. Ask the Holy Spirit to wash away the pain. Ask Jesus to fill your heart with his love.

- Take a look at the specifics. For each accusation, feeling or reaction, proclaim freedom. Release the prisoners, as it were. Let nothing be left there that would entice you to raise any accusation anew.

- Define the realm of trust. Forgiving an offense does not automatically restore trust. If you have been cheated or abused, then you may need to define boundaries which will help prevent the offense from repeating itself. But these boundaries should be erected without employing rejection. It should be done in a way that promotes peace and restoration. For example, I have forgiven the thief who once broke into my home. I am not out to see him punished and I would not reject him if I met him on the street. But I did install a better lock on the door through which he entered.

- Bless the offender. Speak blessings over the person. Bless them with the opposite of what has hurt or offended you. In the realm of grace, there is no such thing as an undeserved blessing.

Our father sends his rain on the righteous as well as the unrighteous. In other words, it is his nature to pour out blessings. And he invites us to learn to walk in that same nature. This is what it means to be a son or daughter—growing into a reflection of the heart of the Father.

The Walk of the Child
Being a Peacemaker

Now, this is the goal: to live in harmony with one another and demonstrate affectionate love, sympathy, and kindness toward other believers. Let humility describe who you are as you dearly love one another. Never retaliate when someone treats you wrongly, nor insult those who insult you, but instead, respond by speaking a blessing over them—because a blessing is what God promised to give you.

(1 PET 3:8–9 TPT)

5

What is Peace?

THE HEBREW WORD FOR peace, *shalom*, is a very rich word. It can mean completeness, prosperity, safety, tranquility, soundness, welfare, health, contentment, and friendship. A peacemaker is a person who walks in the full breadth of this richness.

In the following chapters we will look at several realms of peace. We'll look at how these things can pervade our own lives, and how we can live so that these realms influence those with whom we interact, as well as influencing society at large.

The realms we will look at are:

- freedom from the political spirit
- freedom from war
- freedom from violence and criminality
- economic security
- freedom from lies, deception and accusation
- freedom from demonic influences
- freedom from conflict
- freedom from worry
- a haven of blessing and rest
- true identity
- health and strength
- the tangible presence of God

The Walk of the Child

That's a pretty broad spectrum, ranging from international politics, through interpersonal relationships, to inner healing and personal wellbeing. Which means there might be some points where you disagree with me, and where I haven't necessarily gone into enough depth to make a thorough case. Be that as it may.

As we look at these realms, especially the realms where politics play a role, it is important to remember that this is a book about being a child and a peacemaker. We will touch on things that may be biblically permissible, and yet are not in line with the heart of the Father.

That may seem strange to you. Most of us are so accustomed to reading the Bible from a knowledge of good and evil perspective, that we tend to interpret it in terms of what is permitted or forbidden. But there are things which God has permitted as a concession, dare I say compromise, even though they are *not* his will or his desire.

The clearest example is divorce. The Law of Moses permits a man to divorce his wife. Jesus says that his Father made this concession, despite it being a violation of his intent, his heart and his will.[1]

But there are other examples as well. Jesus did only what he saw his Father doing. Which means that Jesus lived his life in a way that demonstrated what lies on his Father's heart. And yet, much of his interaction with the religious leaders of the day demonstrated the distance between what the Law allowed and where the Father's heart actually lay.

This became even more evident after The Great Shift, which has again opened the way for us to eat of the Tree of Life rather than the knowledge of good and evil. It is possible to build a biblically sound theology permitting or forbidding things which are inconsistent with the longings of God's heart. The Sermon on the Mount gives us many such examples. Jesus did not preach that sermon in order to give us a more demanding law. Rather he portrayed several examples of how things which are biblically permissible turn out to not be in alignment with the heart of the Father. The love of the Father invites us to live in accordance with his heart rather than just within the boundaries of what he has permitted.

---

1. See Matt 19:3–8 and Mark 10:2–9

What is Peace?

The Nature of Peace

As Jesus implied in the Sermon on the Mount: You will be revealed as a son or daughter of your Father in heaven, through living out the same values which he holds dear.[2]

Which raises the question: What are the values that he holds dear? The Law and the Prophets tell us quite a bit about the nature of God, but they give us only occasional glimpses into the longings of his heart.

There are four passages in the New Testament which speak specifically about what God longs for. I believe that these passages are a significant window into the values at the core of his heart.

He Wants All People to Be Saved

> This is good, and pleases God our Savior, who wants all people to be saved and to come to a knowledge of the truth. (1 Tim 2:3–4)

He *wants* all people to be saved and learn to know the truth. There is nobody who is not included in "all people." We are all his children—both those who walk in relationship to him and those who do not (yet) know him to be Truth. There is no limit to the lengths to which he will go to see his children restored to relationship with him. This desire is very inclusive: there is nobody whom he wishes to see excluded.

He Longs to Dwell in Us

> Or do you think that the Scripture speaks to no purpose: "He jealously desires the Spirit which He has made to dwell in us"? (Jas 4:5 NASB)

He *longs* for his Spirit to dwell in his children. I believe that this longing encompasses much more than us being spirit-filled. It involves us becoming so inhabited by the ways of the Spirit that there is no conflict or imbalance between his ways and our ways. And this longing applies to all of his children, even those whom we may consider to be wicked.

---

2. See Matt 5:43–45. See also John 15:13, Rom 5:8, 1 Tim 1:16, 1 John 2:6, and 1 John 3:16

The Walk of the Child

He Seeks Worshipers

> Yet a time is coming and has now come when the true worshipers will worship the Father in the Spirit and in truth, for they are the kind of worshipers the Father seeks. (John 4:23)

He *seeks* worshipers who worship in the Spirit and in truth. Father God is not looking for servants or for worshipers who worship only in word or in deed. He has very little pleasure in ritual activities. He longs for intimacy with sons and daughters (worshipers) who allow his Spirit and his Truth to dwell in them. He longs for his children to be living expressions of his nature.

He Desires Unity

> My prayer is not for them alone. I pray also for those who will believe in me through their message, that all of them may be one, Father, just as you are in me and I am in you. May they also be in us so that the world may believe that you have sent me. I have given them the glory that you gave me, that they may be one as we are one—I in them and you in me—so that they may be brought to complete unity. Then the world will know that you sent me and have loved them even as you have loved me. Father, I want those you have given me to be with me where I am, and to see my glory, the glory you have given me because you loved me before the creation of the world. (John 17:20-24)

He *desires* to join with his bride in unity. Unity is not defined by uniformity of thought or belief. Unity is entirely relational. Love is demonstrated by how you treat those with whom you disagree. There is no better example of this than Father God who rains blessing on the evil and the unrighteous.

Incorporating these things into our lives will impact our preferences and our values and our politics. Living as a peacemaker will necessitate adopting the culture of the Kingdom of Heaven, and may actually bring us into cross-purposes with the culture of our society.

Peacemaking

Peacemaking involves influencing both those around us and the culture in which we live, in a way that leads to growth for each of these realms of

What is Peace?

peace at which we will look. Among other things, it involves changing the atmosphere in the culture so that those spiritual influences which restrict peace will lose their grip.

Put another way, the so-called Great Commission[3] is a call to peacemaking. The call to make disciples of all nations is much more than a call to see people from every nation make a decision for Christ. To disciple is to train, to nurture, and to teach. A disciple is someone who intently follows the ways of their teacher. So to disciple a nation is to train and influence that society in a way that brings about a change in culture.

This is why Jesus said that he would build his *ekklesia*.[4] It is worth noting that he did not say he would build his temple or his synagogue, the two established religious institutions of the day. Instead, Jesus used a word with no religious connotations at all.

The Greek word *ekklesia* is usually translated to English as church. But that is an inaccurate translation. In the original language, the word is used to describe a crowd or a group of people set apart for a specific purpose. In the Roman empire of Jesus' day, the word *ekklesia* was frequently used to describe an assembly of influential people in a newly conquered community, who were tasked with establishing the culture of the empire in that community.

In other words, Jesus did not so much say that he would build his church, as he said that he would build a movement of people whose calling was to influence the society where they live so that it adopts the ways and the culture of the Kingdom of Heaven. This is not done by forcing the community to obey a set of rules, but by creating an atmosphere which enables the community to rise up to the calling for which it was created, just as the yeast mixed through a bread dough causes the dough to rise.[5]

When the *ekklesia* is living out the culture of the Kingdom of Heaven in a visible and attractive manner, then the community will be lifted up. It is not the handful of truly evil people in a community that prevent changing the atmosphere. The real hindrance is when the majority of Christians in a community are mostly good, but not quite living a Kingdom lifestyle. Peacemaking is more than just living peacefully.

---

3. Matt 28:19–20

4. See Matthew 16:18. A comprehensive look at the subject of *ekklesia* is beyond the scope of this book. For a deeper understanding, I highly recommend the book *Ekklesia*, by Ed Silvoso.

5. See Matt 13:33 or Luke 13:21

> In the same way, let your light shine before others, that they may see your good deeds and glorify your Father in heaven. (Matt 5:16)

"God is light; in him there is no darkness at all."[6] This is exactly the mechanism we need in order to experience the whole measure of the fullness of Christ.[7] We should not accept that there be any room for any form of darkness in us or in our society. Our calling is for all of the darkness to be purified away, so that only gold, silver, and jewels remain.[8]

You may be thinking now of spiritual warfare, and in a sense that is what is needed. But the term spiritual warfare may be a bit misleading. In the spiritual realm, a stronghold is defeated by walking in the opposite spirit. So warfare, in the military sense, will never succeed in driving out the spiritual forces that are opposed to peace. Neither anger, nor force, nor aggression, nor rules are suitable tools for the peacemaker. Whatever it may look like at the outset, that which is established with such tools will not turn out to be peace in the long run.

The Journey

The following chapters are written from a desire to communicate the heart of Father God, who is Love. The Call of the Child is to reflect the nature of their Father. Which, as Jesus pointed out in the Sermon on the Mount, leads us to being peacemakers. As peacemakers, we are called to look at each of these realms of peace through the eyes of the Prince of Peace, to gain his perspective and move in step with his heartbeat.

I still have much to learn in the ways of the Kingdom. Though I have some degree of experience and authority in several of these realms of peace, there is still more to be gained. The road to being a peacemaker is a journey of discovery where the reward is a glorious family likeness to our Good and Loving Father. It is a journey of a child walking hand in hand with Father—not a mission to be carried out through our own efforts or desires. As children, we are not meant to walk alone.

Our enemy, the destroyer, opposes peace by fomenting division and separation, primarily through two means: the religious spirit and the political spirit. Whether these "spirits" are demons or principalities or modes of

---

6. 1 John 1:5
7. See Eph 4:13
8. See 1 Cor 3:12–13

operation or whatever, really does not matter. They are aggressively intent on destroying peace, so we must not be ignorant of their ways.

The religious spirit encourages separation between Father God and his children by either enticing people to worship that which is not God, or by encouraging practices and behaviors of worship that inhibit relationship with God. Its workings are rooted in the knowledge of good and evil, as we saw in chapter 3.

The political spirit sows division and separation between individuals, communities, nations, cultures, and races. So we will start our journey through the realms of peace by looking at how that spirit works.

6

Freedom from the Political Spirit

> Make every effort to keep the unity of the Spirit through the bond of peace. So Christ himself gave the apostles, the prophets, the evangelists, the pastors and teachers, to equip his people for works of service, so that the body of Christ may be built up until we all reach unity in the faith and in the knowledge of the Son of God and become mature, attaining to the whole measure of the fullness of Christ.
>
> (EPH 4:3, 11–13)

PEACE AND UNITY ARE closely related. In this passage, Paul writes that our Lord has given gifts in order that we might be equipped to maintain the unity of the Spirit. Those gifts are people. People with very different kinds of personalities.

Imagine if you will an apostle, a prophet, an evangelist, a pastor and a teacher sitting together around a table. Those five very different giftings are usually embodied in five very different personalities, which could easily lead to an argument, or at least some misunderstandings. It could turn out to look something like this:

The prophet might get frustrated with or even condemn anyone who doesn't quite see things in the same way that he does, while the teacher could easily be so fixated on some interesting tidbit of truth that he loses touch with the issues at hand. The apostle, a systems thinker, might tend to focus on the big picture and then be consumed with fulfilling that vision, while the pastor may struggle to see beyond the pain and needs of the individuals. And it probably wouldn't be surprising to find that the evangelist got impatient and ran off to share the Gospel with someone.

And yet, in this passage Paul writes that these very different perspectives, working together in harmony, build unity and maturity in the body of believers. In other words, real and practical unity is an essential ingredient in the growth and maturity of the church in the city (and in the world). Yet, as the above example implies, true unity can only work in an atmosphere of love and peace.

So, what is unity? Unity is not uniformity of thought or uniformity of belief or of perspective or behavior. Unity is demonstrated through how we relate to one another in all of our diversity.

Our model for unity is found in how Father, Son and Holy Spirit relate to one another. The Son speaks only what he hears the Father say and does only what he sees the Father do. Likewise with the Spirit, who receives from the Son. And the Son is exalted by the Father.[1] In other words, everything they do with one another is wrapped in lifting one another up, honoring one another, and preferring one another.

That model is perhaps a bit more difficult to put into practice between humans. But the ideal should still apply. Even if the other party doesn't treat me well, I can still relate to them with honor and respect. In fact, I really don't have authority to behave in any other way. In the end, love is measured by how we treat those with whom we disagree and how we honor those who mistreat us. Or as Paul wrote: "If it is possible, as far as it depends on you, live at peace with everyone."[2]

The Political Spirit

Unity is powerful, and consequently something which the enemy of our souls is intent on destroying. The political spirit is perhaps the primary mechanism for damaging and destroying relationships between people.

In its most blatant form, the political spirit leads us to think and act out the premise that those with whom I disagree are wrong, are my enemies, and thereby have no value. But it is also a very subtle spirit, which

---

[1]. See John 5:19–23, 8:28, 12:49, 14:10, 16:13, and 16:15, Eph 1:20, Col 3:1, Phil 2:9, and Heb 1:2–8 and 2:9.

[2]. Rom 12:18

The Walk of the Child

works to deceive us into conflict and division, also in small and seemingly inconsequential ways.

Any time we encounter an us and them situation, we need to be aware of the workings of the political spirit. The simple act of defining an "us" means that we are implicitly excluding (and thereby devaluing) "them." It is a subtle kind of division, but it creates fertile ground in which the seeds of estrangement and hatred may grow. And the political spirit thrives on that.

An us and them perspective might seem logical, rational, or even biblical, especially from a knowledge of good and evil perspective. Even the psalmist David sometimes took such a position, like when he wrote, "Do I not hate those who hate you?"[3]

But there is no room for thinking us and them in a Tree of Life framework. There is no call for division after The Great Shift. Grace calls us to look at people, not based on what they think or what they do, but rather based on their potential and what they are created to be. And we are all created (whether we believe or not) to be sons and daughters of Father God and a united bride of Jesus.

When Father God looks at a person (be they one of us or one of them), he sees his child, whom he loves with unfailing love. That person may be anywhere from completely rebellious to lost to confused to obedient to intimately close. But none of those things can change the measure of Father's love for that person. He doesn't see them as being in or out. Instead, he sees his child whom he loves and longs to embrace. He is the God who pours out blessing on both the good and the evil.

> You have heard that it was said, "Love your neighbor and hate your enemy." But I tell you, love your enemies and pray for those who persecute you, that you may be children of your Father in heaven. He causes his sun to rise on the evil and the good, and sends rain on the righteous and the unrighteous. For if you love those who love you, what reward do you have? Do not even the tax collectors do the same? If you greet only your brothers, what more are you doing than others? Do not even the Gentiles do the same? (Matt 5:43–47)

This passage sums up The Call of the Child. It is all about how a mature son or daughter of Father God behaves when facing the political spirit. Jesus is saying that his Father loves those who hate him, and that mature children of the Father will do likewise.

---

3. Ps 139:21–22

This is the way of The Great Shift, where mercy triumphs over judgment. This is the way of the Tree of Life, when the knowledge of good and evil would entice us to condemn and devalue those who (in our eyes) do wrong. This is the way of forgiveness, which raises no claim even when wronged.

Ambition

> Do nothing out of selfish ambition or vain conceit. Rather, in humility value others above yourselves, not looking to your own interests but each of you to the interests of the others. (Phil 2:3–4)

In this passage, Paul calls us to say no to the political spirit and rather clothe ourselves in the ways of Jesus and the Principle of the Cross. Vain conceit is pride; the core attitude in the enemy's corrupted wisdom. Selfish ambition is using whatever means available to gain position or authority; the core attitude of the political spirit.

Selfish ambition is not a good thing. In fact, I am tempted to write that ambition is not a good thing—at least in nearly all cases;[4] because ambition is rooted in our own efforts. Ambitions are seldom achieved through unity.

The Passion Translation makes this even clearer:

> Be free from pride-filled opinions, for they will only harm your cherished unity. (Phil 2:3a TPT)

It is not wrong to have dreams or goals. In fact, each of us is created with a destiny or a purpose or a birthright, which is planted deep in who we are. The things we dream of becoming or achieving are a window into that destiny. And Father God desires to see those dreams fulfilled in our lives. But if we try to get there on our own, we might very easily end up partnering with the political spirit.

That's what happened with the prodigal son. He was a son in his father's house. He had a birthright and a purpose. And part of that included celebration. But rather than walking together with his father into his destiny, he chose to try to get there alone. At first it seemed like he had come into a lifestyle of celebration, but that didn't last for long. Along the way there

---

4. Selfish ambition is the NIV translation of the Greek word *eritheia*. The NIV also translates the Greek word *philotimeomai* (which implies honorably aiming at a goal—a very different thing from how ambition usually looks) as ambition in a couple of cases, while other translations use strive, labor, or aspire for *philotimeomai*.

was a lot of pain, loss and separation. And then he came to himself and once again looked toward his father—who received him with celebration.

Many a gifted Christian has gained a vision of the call upon their life and the destiny which Father has prepared for them. And yet, somewhere along the way, the dream becomes an ambition and (usually without realizing it) they trade out the Father's hand with the deceitful encouragement of the political spirit. It is a recipe for shipwreck, and there is usually a lot of destruction along the way.

The political spirit will often grant what appears to be success and victory along the way. Because that spirit has a tendency to think long-term. For example, an ambitious pastor's congregation may experience that many people come to faith and perhaps see dramatic healing and deliverance. While at the same time a cancerous culture of control or fear is lurking under the surface, waiting for the right time to explode.

Which is why we do well to remember Paul's admonition to value others above yourself and prefer their interests over your own. With that attitude, there is no us and them to give the political spirit a foothold.

Sowing Rebellion

The term political spirit can be a bit misleading, because it is by no means limited only to the political arena. You could almost say: Where two or three are gathered, there the political spirit would like to sow division. For example, it has played a role in the beginnings of many protestant denominations. So even though the remainder of this chapter looks at its role in the realm of government, the principles apply in almost any area of social interaction.

> Let everyone be subject to the governing authorities, for there is no authority except that which God has established. The authorities that exist have been established by God. Consequently, whoever rebels against the authority is rebelling against what God has instituted, and those who do so will bring judgment on themselves. (Rom 13:1-2)

For the most part, the kingdoms of this world are influenced by the enemy of our souls, despite their authority having been ordained by God. You may not find it easy to wrap your mind around that. We might think that, if God is in it then it must be right. And yet, that is not always the case. Paul wrote his letter to the Romans during the reign of Caesar Nero. And,

Freedom from the Political Spirit

implicitly, Paul said that Caesar's authority (which he used to persecute Christians) was ordained of God.

Does that mean that God ordains the evil that a bad government may dish out? I think not. Paul wrote his letter to believers, and in the context of chapter 13, he is writing about how we as sons and daughters of the Living God are to relate to our government and our society.

The authority of a government is ordained by God. Without authority, a government can not govern. God gives authority to a government. It is a gift. And God does not revoke his gifts,[5] even though they may be misused.

Paul wrote that to rebel against the authority of a government is a sin with dire consequences. In light of the ungodly government that was in place at the time of Paul's writing, his instruction remains true even though we may feel that our own government is illegitimate.

I am fully aware that such a statement may not sit well with the American reader. The United States was founded through acts of violent rebellion against the governing authority of the time. The Declaration of Independence is a cherished American document, which eloquently lays a case to justify the rebellion. The grievances it lists are valid and serious. Yet it still violates Paul's instruction in the first verses of Romans 13.

Traditional American Christian history teaches us that the nation's founding fathers were men of faith, that God blessed the American colonies, and that the successful outcome of the American revolutionary war (against a far superior military power) was a miracle. In general, I believe those things to be largely true. But the blessings of God are not necessarily a measure of God's approval. He is, after all, the God who pours out his blessings on both the righteous and the unrighteous.

So what happened? It seems to me that, as colonial dissatisfaction grew over how the government in England treated them, the political spirit found opportunity to sow division. The colonials began to view the government in England as illegitimate. This spirit went on to discourage people on both sides of the split from negotiating and reaching compromise. That eventually led to an act of rebellion and a war that cost many lives. A great nation was born out of this, but at the cost of a loss of peace. A price which I believe still influences the nation to this day, as we shall see in the following chapters.

The seeds of rebellion foster polarization. Society finds itself divided into those who rebel and those who remain loyal. Distrust can then grow into hatred between the two camps. And violence follows quickly after.

---

5. See Rom 11:29

The Walk of the Child

My son-in-law once gave me a book about the decay of democratic government and how it might be prevented. The authors, two Harvard political science professors, identify a couple of norms by which a democracy remains healthy. When these norms break down then it is quite likely that the government will become autocratic or dictatorial. Although these authors don't use my terminology, their description of the breakdown of democratic norms is an excellent description of the workings of the political spirit. A couple of quotes:

> "The weakening of our democratic norms is rooted in extreme partisan polarization—one that extends beyond policy differences into an existential conflict over race and culture."[6]

> "If we view our rivals as a dangerous threat, we have much to fear if they are elected. We may decide to employ any means necessary to defeat them—and therein lies a justification for authoritarian measures."[7]

One of the troubling aspects of this polarization, is how tightly it seems to be coupled to racism and nationalism. The us and them mentality can be frighteningly comfortable and attractive. It can even be justified with a selective use of biblical scriptures. But such division is not in alignment with the heart of Father God, who wants all people to be saved.[8] Central to our calling as sons and daughters of a Good Father is that we live lives and build relationships which not only avoid but also actively work to extinguish polarization.

> "The most effective coalitions are those that bring together groups with dissimilar—even opposing—views on many issues. They are built not among friends but among adversaries."[9]

The political spirit deludes us to value ideology over relationship and consequently power over peace. This is dangerous stuff that, in the long term, leads only to bondage and destruction. The peacemaker will do well to look beyond quick solutions and rather have their gaze fixed on those things which grow from the Tree of Life.

---

6. Levitsky and Ziblatt, *How Democracies Die*, 9.
7. Levitsky and Ziblatt, *How Democracies Die*, 104.
8. See 1 Tim 2:3–4
9. Levitsky and Ziblatt, *How Democracies Die*, 218–19.

The Role of Government

The question remains: What about bad governments? Is it really God's will that his people should live under an oppressive or wicked government? Definitely not.

We are called to pray that the Kingdom of God would come and his will be done here on Earth as it is in Heaven. But we are *not* called to use the tools of rebellion or in any way allow the political spirit to influence us as we may pray for a change of government. That is not the way of God. Violating the Principle of the Cross to bring about a change of authority will always have a high price.

One of the big differences which I have observed between American culture and Norwegian culture is how government is viewed.

Norwegians, for the most part, trust their government and are happy to let the government manage many areas of their lives. Although the tax level is fairly high, most pay their taxes willingly. Every spring, the tax authorities upload each person's tax return to their personal online account, already filled out (since nearly all relevant information is available to the government), for taxpayers to check (and correct, if necessary) the numbers. Most Norwegians are happy with that system, which they consider easy, accurate and fair.

Americans, however, are generally skeptical to government and for the most part reluctant or downright opposed to paying taxes. Many do not trust their government and do not want the government involved in areas which they consider to be their private sphere. If American tax authorities were to try implementing a tax return system similar to that in Norway, it would not surprise me if violence broke out.

I suspect that American distrust of government has its roots in the rebellion by which the nation was founded. Although independence and self-sufficiency are highly valued in American culture, Father God did not create us to be driven by such attitudes. He created us to be dependent on one another, much in the same manner that the various parts of a body must interact in order to function properly.[10]

> Do everything without grumbling or arguing, so that you may become blameless and pure, "children of God without fault in a warped and crooked generation." Then you will shine among them like stars in the sky as you hold firmly to the word of life. (Phil 2:14–16a)

---

10. See 1 Cor 12:12–26

The Walk of the Child

I do not believe that distrust and skepticism are healthy attitudes—they are variants of grumbling and arguing. The Philippians, to whom Paul wrote, lived under a far more repressive and ungodly regime than any modern democracy. As children we are called to trust. As Christians we are called to bless and to not curse—even in the face of bad or wicked governments. Expressions of distrust are often thinly veiled curses. Distrust seldom evokes blessing. When God's people cease to be a people of blessing, the voice of the political spirit is more widely heard.

The Lord spoke a crucial word[11] through the prophet Jeremiah:

> Hear the word of the LORD to you, king of Judah, you who sit on David's throne—you, your officials and your people who come through these gates. This is what the LORD says: Do what is just and right. Rescue from the hand of the oppressor the one who has been robbed. Do no wrong or violence to the foreigner, the fatherless or the widow, and do not shed innocent blood in this place. For if you are careful to carry out these commands, then kings who sit on David's throne will come through the gates of this palace, riding in chariots and on horses, accompanied by their officials and their people. But if you do not obey these commands, declares the LORD, I swear by myself that this palace will become a ruin. (Jer 22:2–5)

This passage carries both an admonition and a promise:

- The role of government is to insure peace, especially for the weakest people in society.
- A government which fails to do so will not last.

The promise is that God will not allow an evil government to last. The challenge for the peacemaker is to trust God's timing in that respect. I truly believe that God's first choice is to see a government change from within, rather than forcing a change of government. This is implicit in the word spoken through Jeremiah: Please change your heart so that you govern well, so that I may continue to bless you rather than being compelled to bring change by my own hand.

The peacemaker can do much to influence society and to change the spiritual climate there. We will look at several examples in the following

---

11. This is not an isolated word, but a recurring theme throughout the Law and the Prophets. Father God is especially fond of widows, orphans, and foreigners; and their welfare is dear to his heart.

chapters. It takes time; perhaps more than a lifetime. But the deceptive shortcut offered by the political spirit will always lead to destruction.

7

Freedom from War

> Too long have I lived among those who hate peace. I am for peace;
> but when I speak, they are for war.
>
> (PS 120:6–7)

For those who live in a combat zone, war is a total breakdown of peace. So much so that most of the other realms of peace become comparatively irrelevant in a society wracked by war. Therefore, it is fundamental to the calling of a peacemaker to pursue freedom from war.

War Is a Bad Thing

As I mentioned in the introduction, my father was a U. S. military officer. But, like many servicemen of his (and my) generation, he never saw actual combat duty. He was only seventeen when World War II ended, and his tours of duty did not take him into any of the combat regions of the Cold War era. So, despite over thirty years of active service, his first-hand relationship to war was not very unlike that of most American civilians.

For most Americans, war is something that happens somewhere else. There has not been any international military combat within the boundaries of any U. S. state for more than a hundred years.[1] Both world wars took

---

1. There have been a few combat incidents in U. S. possessions or territories, but those within Alaska and Hawaii took place before these territories became states.

place on other continents, and the wars in which the U. S. has been involved since that time have been waged within the territory of other countries. Which means that, in general, an American's exposure to war is mostly through television, books and films—and that kind of exposure often communicates something very different from the actual horror of war.

It wasn't until after I moved to Europe that I started to realize the significance of this. A substantial part of World War II was fought in Europe, and the signs of destruction were still visible, even after forty-five years or so. Norway (where I now live) was occupied by the Germans, and I eventually came to know several people who had lived through that war. I began to understand, in a way which I had not previously encountered, that war is a really traumatic and destructive thing.

The Old Testament describes the consequences of war with frightening atrocity. Warriors fell by the sword. Homes were looted and burned. Girls were abducted. Women were violated. Pregnant women were ripped open. Infants and children were dashed to pieces. All of this done in hand-to-hand combat. Blood flowed like rivers. Cities and towns were left desolate. To steal, kill, and destroy—these are actions Jesus associated with the devil and with those under the devil's influence.[2]

Things are not that much different today. Although there are international conventions which dictate that civilians should be spared the ravages of military conflict, these are fairly empty words for those who find their lives in the midst of a battle zone. Civilians still end up dead, homes are still looted and burned, and cities and towns are still left desolate. But, unlike Old Testament times, these things can now be done from the safety of an aircraft cockpit or a drone control room.

And then, there is the ultimate weapon (at least, so far). A four megaton hydrogen bomb[3] would vaporize everything within a one mile radius, release enough radiation to rapidly kill everyone within nearly two miles, flatten all buildings within nearly three miles, level most structures within six miles, and spread nuclear fallout over hundreds of miles. This fallout would lead to sickness and eventually a tormenting death for thousands or perhaps millions of people. That is a lot of wanton destruction.

War is a bad thing.

---

2. See John 10:10

3. The largest bomb ever built was fifty megatons! The largest bomb in the U. S. arsenal (after retirement in 2011 of the nine megaton B53) is "only" 1.2 megatons. And the U. S. has more than four thousand combat-ready nuclear warheads.

The Walk of the Child

War in the Old Testament

Much of the Old Testament is the history of the descendants of Abraham living among many other people groups in the region we now call the Middle East. That history is filled with wars, skirmishes, and raiding. Lots of people were killed, looted, and mistreated. Often the motives were empire building, theft, and/or various forms of racism or nationalism.

What I find challenging in all of this, is that it often seems as though much of this military conflict had God's approval. After wandering forty years in the desert, the descendants of Israel were commanded to conquer and annihilate the inhabitants of the land and then take possession of it. And it seems that God frequently used raiding armies to punish this same people as they drifted away from faithfully following their God. So it is not difficult, from an Old Testament perspective, to build a theological case in support of waging war.

There are, however, a few indications in the Old Testament framework that give us some hints that war is not really the way of the Kingdom of God. Some of the most dramatic victories actually came about without combat, such as when the armies besieging Jerusalem fled in the middle of the night, or when worshipers were sent out to lead the armies.

To me, one of the strongest indicators is that King David was disqualified from building the temple of God because he was a man of blood. The dwelling place of God is not meant to be laid on a foundation of warfare. And we, his children, are created to be that dwelling place.

I believe that God's seeming approval of Old Testament warfare is a consequence of a society operating under the knowledge of good and evil, prior to The Great Shift. And I am convinced that when Jesus taught us to pray that the Kingdom of God should come on Earth as it is in Heaven, he was also teaching us to pray for an end to warfare.

Three Streams

There are three main theological streams in modern Christianity concerning war. Simply put, they are:[4]

- *Pacifist*: War is always wrong.

---

4. It is beyond the scope of this book to delve deeply into these streams. The reader is encouraged to investigate the wealth of resources available which discuss Christian pacifism and/or the Just War tradition.

- *Nationalist*: War is acceptable when it is in the interests of the nation waging war.
- *Just War*: War is acceptable when necessary to prevent an even worse condition. There must be a morally justifiable reason for going to war, and war must be waged in a morally just manner.

This being a book about peace, I am (not surprisingly) writing from a pacifist perspective. It is not my intent to say that other perspectives are wrong. But I truly believe that a pacifist perspective is closely aligned with the Father's heart.

I am fully aware that Christian pacifism is a minority perspective in our time, at least in Western Christianity. Most Christians would probably say that they embrace the Just War perspective, although in practice many may actually lean farther toward a nationalist perspective than they might like to admit.

The first expressions of a Just War tradition pre-date Christianity. There are writings from ancient India, Egypt and Rome which describe aspects of Just War philosophy. But such thinking did not greatly influence those cultures.

Augustine of Hippo was the first Christian teacher to formulate a Just War theology; and he did so in the fourth century. Prior to that time, it looks as though all Christian teaching embraced the pacifist perspective. Some, such as Hippolytus of Rome, went so far as to espouse denying baptism to soldiers who did not resign their commission.

I find it interesting, and perhaps unsettling, that mainstream Christian theology transitioned from being pacifist to taking a Just War perspective in the same time frame that Christianity (at least within the Roman empire) transitioned from an underground framework to an institutional and state-entangled structure. I suspect that this transition has influenced the church in ways which have led to theological positions in our day which the apostles and early church fathers would hardly recognize.

War in the New Testament

The teachings of Jesus and the writings of the Apostles do not speak specifically about waging war—with two exceptions:

- In Luke 14:31, while teaching about counting the cost, Jesus uses an example of a king contemplating war.

The Walk of the Child

- In 2 Cor 10:3, Paul writes that we do not wage war as the world does.

But the teaching and lifestyle of Jesus is filled with examples of non-violent attitudes, even at the cost of personal loss. Behaviors such as loving your enemies, turning the other cheek, blessing instead of cursing, not repaying evil for evil, and so on, are found throughout the New Testament.

There are, however, a couple of New Testament passages which refer to the sword and which are sometimes used to justify war in this age. I do not believe that either of these passages are sufficient to support a Just War or Nationalist theological perspective.

Swords at Jesus' Arrest

Luke (in chapter 22) describes Jesus talking to his disciples at the end of the Last Supper, a few hours prior to his arrest. He explains to them that things are about to change (verses 31–36). While Jesus was with them, they experienced supernatural provision which made faithfully following him relatively easy. But henceforth their faith was to be tested in the absence of such provision. And in that context, Jesus said, "If you don't have a sword . . . buy one."

In verse 37, Jesus quoted a prophesy from Isaiah 53, that he would be found among transgressors. In other words, he would be found in the company of lawbreakers. Which leads me to conclude that he mentioned buying swords in connection with being found in such company.

In verse 38, the disciples tell him that they have two swords, to which Jesus replies, "That's enough!" It is possible to interpret Jesus as having said something like, "Yes, two swords are enough for our purposes." But, in the context here, it seems more likely to me that Jesus was saying something more along the lines of, "Enough talk about swords—I am speaking figuratively here."

Later the same evening, when Jesus was arrested (verses 49–51), he strongly rebuked his disciples for using their swords, and then healed the injured party.

In light of this context, I believe that this passage clearly demonstrates Jesus' disapproval of the use of the sword. As I see it, this passage does not support using the sword for waging war nor even for purposes of self defense.[5]

---

5. We'll return to the subject of self defense in the following chapter.

Freedom from War

Bearing the Sword

> Let everyone be subject to the governing authorities, for there is no authority except that which God has established. The authorities that exist have been established by God. Consequently, whoever rebels against the authority is rebelling against what God has instituted, and those who do so will bring judgment on themselves. For rulers hold no terror for those who do right, but for those who do wrong. Do you want to be free from fear of the one in authority? Then do what is right and you will be commended. For the one in authority is God's servant for your good. But if you do wrong, be afraid, for rulers do not bear the sword for no reason. They are God's servants, agents of wrath to bring punishment on the wrongdoer. Therefore, it is necessary to submit to the authorities, not only because of possible punishment but also as a matter of conscience. This is also why you pay taxes, for the authorities are God's servants, who give their full time to governing. Give to everyone what you owe them: If you owe taxes, pay taxes; if revenue, then revenue; if respect, then respect; if honor, then honor. (Rom 13:1–7)

Augustine of Hippo leaned heavily on this passage in framing his Just War theology. However, I disagree with Augustine's interpretation.

This passage is within the context (chapters 12 and 13) of how we as believers should relate to other people. The dominant theme through these two chapters is to not repay evil for evil, for love does no harm to a neighbor. And in that context, these seven verses are primarily about not being in rebellion to the ruling government.

As we saw in the previous chapter, God-ordained authority does not give a government a blank check. The purpose of government is to insure peace, and a government which fails to do so will not last. While verse 4 does acknowledge the role of government to punish lawbreakers, I do not believe this passage can be stretched to the point where it implies that God ordains war-mongering.

For about three hundred years after the death of Jesus, his followers refused to act violently. Soldiers who came to faith typically resigned their positions, sometimes at the cost of their own lives. Even today, those who suffer persecution for their Christian faith rarely respond with violence.[6] Warfare is not the way of the Kingdom which has drawn near. It is not the

---

6. See the University of Notre Dame report, *Under Caesar's Sword*, at https://ucs.nd.edu

way of the Principle of the Cross. It is not the way of the Tree of Life. There is no place for it in a culture of freedom.

The Full Armor of God

Now you may be thinking of the several biblical passages which describe our God as a Mighty Warrior or which use a warfare paradigm to illustrate some aspect of the ways of the Kingdom. I believe that all such passages need to be interpreted in light of what Jesus did on the Cross.

> For though we live in the world, we do not wage war as the world does. The weapons we fight with are not the weapons of the world. On the contrary, they have divine power to demolish strongholds. We demolish arguments and every pretension that sets itself up against the knowledge of God, and we take captive every thought to make it obedient to Christ. (2 Cor 10:3–5)

In these verses, Paul makes it very clear that it is not the place of a Christian to wage war as the world does, or to employ the things which the world calls weapons. Rather, where the Christian does fight for something, it is for the purpose of bringing (usually our own) thoughts and attitudes into line with the ways of the Kingdom of God. And the weapons for this kind of battle are the belt of truth, the breastplate of righteousness, the gospel of peace, the shield of faith, the helmet of salvation, and the sword of the Spirit which is the word of God.[7] None of these weapons can be used to kill a person, but they are the most powerful weapons available for overcoming evil. The weakness of God is stronger than human strength.[8]

We may read these words from 2 Corinthians and think that they are symbolic, a good image for how the individual believer can stand against the onslaught of sin and unrighteousness in our individual lives. And that is true.

But can we really say that this call to not wage war as the world does only applies to our personal lives, and not to the nation in which we live? Does it make sense to carry the shield of faith on a personal level, and yet be driven by fear on a national level? Father God is not segmented like that, and neither should his children be. Rather, our commission to disciple nations calls us to influence the nation in which we live so that it will not wage war as the world does.

---

7. See Eph 6:10–17
8. See 1 Cor 1:25

Freedom from War

The weapons with which we fight are powerful to demolish every pretension that sets itself up against the knowledge of God. With them, we can expose the lies of the knowledge of good and evil and reveal the truth of the Father's love for every person.

This is where the belt of truth comes in. Our thoughts and our words are to be encompassed by the Father's truth. The fruit of the Tree of Life is powerful for releasing people into freedom. Exposing the lies of the devil and establishing the truth of Father God's unbounded love for the world[9] has enormous power to release peace, not only for the individual but also for a nation.

The breastplate of righteousness covers the heart. As a result of The Great Shift, there is no longer any condemnation for sins. The price has been paid. A nation which embraces this revelation will find no cause for waging war. Instead, their sense of identity, their respect for neighbors and their quickness to forgive will give them such favor in the international community that conflicts will not arise.

Nearly all conflicts, whether interpersonal or international, arise out of an orphan spirit. By orphan spirit I mean the tendency to take control of one's own welfare, needs, safety, or whatever. The gospel of peace is a message that God is a Good Father who cares for and provides for his children. Wars are fought to gain territory, resources, or power when the orphan spirit tells us that we fight for our survival. But the person or nation which hears *and receives* the gospel of peace will be set free from the need to be their own provider and protector.

Before a nation goes to war, it usually needs to drum up support for the conflict among the people of that nation. And fear is perhaps the most effective tool for quickly achieving that goal. A people under the control of fear will easily be persuaded to take steps that they would not even consider when they are in a more rational state of mind. The weapon that destroys fear is the shield of faith. Faith is not an intellectual knowledge or understanding of some religious concept. Faith is rooted in trust. Trusting that God is in control, that nothing escapes his notice, and that nothing can separate you from his love, is the shield of faith. It works for the individual and it can work for the nation. Not only does the peacemaker trust for his or her personal security, but the peacemaker communicates and models trust and confidence in the face of whatever may instill fear in their surroundings.

---

9. See John 3:16–17

The helmet of salvation is similar. It guards the mind from accusations and deceptions, by setting focus on the victory of the cross where the enemy was completely defeated. It reminds us of The Great Shift, where there is nothing to fear and nothing left to defeat. From a perspective of salvation, there is no need for war.

Finally, there is the sword of the Spirit which is the word of God. The Greek word *machaira*, which in this case is translated as sword, is not the word for a long battle sword. It is the word for a short sword or knife or dagger. In battle, such a short sword would often be used to remove arrows or to clean wounds. As such, it is more a tool for healing and restoration than for damage or destruction. Likewise, the peacemaker's use of the Word of God is to bring blessing, healing, restoration and deliverance. This is especially true for how we communicate in the public arena. Blessing, healing and restoration are not only for those on our side but even more necessary for those who we might consider to be against us.

Just War

As previously mentioned, a majority of Christians today (at least in Western nations) embrace the Just War tradition which, although opposed to warfare in general, accepts the necessity of a so-called Just War. Simply put, a war is considered just if combat is unavoidable and necessary to prevent or to bring an end to conditions which are even worse than the horrors of war. The Just War tradition also expects that combat will be carried out with no more violence than necessary.

These are rational concessions, at least in theory. But they are very difficult to maintain in reality. Many wars have been fought since World War II, but none of them would meet the strict standards of being a Just War. Instead, the expediencies of national interest quickly creep in, leading Christians to support, or at least accept, wars that they would be hard pressed to condone theologically.

I grew up not questioning this. After all, during the Cold War, we in America were led to believe that the Communists were out to steal our way of life, and that we needed to defend ourselves. And there was some measure of truth in that. So, as a good American, I was raised to not question the international operations of my country, since it was all for the supposed greater good of saving the world from the evils of communism.

The fallacy there, is to conclude that if communism is evil then those who oppose communism must be good. And if they are good then anything that they do must also be good.

It did not occur to me as I was growing up to wonder what a person living in a communist nation (or any of the countries where cold war combat took place) might think about my country. Would they have reason to fear that my nation might attack them? Would they feel terrorized by the threat of thousands of nuclear warheads standing in readiness to be fired at their homes? Might the only nation that has ever actually used a nuclear weapon in combat (twice) be inclined to do so again? Does a people who has virtually never been on the receiving end of a bombing raid have the capacity to show restraint? Can they fight a Just War?

Even if a war starts out meeting the criteria for a Just War, it will tend to degenerate. War encompasses killing, stealing, and destroying—things which are the domain of the devil. Most people who operate in that domain will be influenced by the spirits of death and destruction.

People are not for killing. We were not created for bloodshed. Causing another person to die—be it accidental, in combat, or murder—has dire consequences for the soul and spirit of the killer. Something inside gets broken or twisted, which will influence that person for the rest of their life. This is one of the reasons so many soldiers come home from combat to find themselves facing PTSD or other challenges.

One of the most common techniques used to make combat palatable, is to dehumanize the enemy. They are usually called something derogatory (such as *gooks* in the Korean and Vietnam wars) and are often portrayed as being evil, as if they don't deserve to live. However, dehumanization encourages combat that exceeds the mandate of a Just War. If those who are being killed deserve to die, then there is no need to minimize the force.

A Peace-Loving Nation

In America, we tend to think of ourselves as a peace-loving nation. But whose peace? Certainly not the peace of the people who live in those countries where U. S. forces have waged war. The peoples of Afghanistan, Somalia, Iraq and Libya are certainly not experiencing more peace today than before they were invaded or bombed.[10]

---

10. It is not my intent here to criticize the soldiers who have been deployed to these combat situations. The issue here is rather the political choices that lead to soldiers being

The Walk of the Child

I understand that international politics is a complex thing, and that there are not easy answers when conflicts arise. However, the strategy of forcefully imposing a regime change on a nation does not result in peace. Even in the case of dictatorships which subject their populations to great evil, going to war does not make things better.

A true peace-loving nation is not only concerned about its own peace, but also about there being peace in all other nations as well. A true peace-loving nation will not force other nations to behave in a certain way, even when another nation may choose to behave badly. Peace does not come about through strength. Peace can not be maintained by force.

> Do not be overcome by evil, but overcome evil with good.
> (Rom 12:21)

In the year or so prior to World War II, Germany invaded neighbors for the purpose of protecting German-speaking minorities, and for protecting Germanic interests. It looked a bit like a Just War, and the church in Germany to a large degree supported it.[11] It seemed like good and noble moves. This eventually led to a war of expansion which occupied much of Europe and ended with the extermination of millions of "undesirable" people, in the name of protecting German interests.

Today, we look back upon these events and see them as evil. But do we recognize that some of the same patterns can be at work in our own time?

America threatens to crush nations who threaten America or its interests. Those nations are portrayed as being evil. And some church leaders all too readily speak out in favor of crushing the evil. But fighting evil with evil has a tendency to only make both parties more evil. This is not what a peace-loving nation is meant to look like.

Nations differ from one another. They have personalities. America has been described as an Adventurous Leader[12] and as a Prophet nation.[13] Such descriptions speak to the nation's calling (the purpose for which it was created) and to a specific expression of the glory that God has planted in each nation.[14] The prophetic leadership calling upon America is, among

placed in combat.

11. There were a minority, probably less than 20 percent, of Christians in Germany who spoke out against the Church's alignment with the Nazi government. Most were persecuted and some, such as Dietrich Bonhoeffer, paid a high price for their opposition.

12. Bos, *The Nations Called*, 128

13. Burk, *Redemptive Gifts of Cities*, CD 2

14. See Rev 21:24

other things, meant to be an expression of God's innovative and redemptive ways of leading people and societies into freedom from the bondage of the knowledge of good and evil. This calling was never meant to be wasted on becoming a leader in killing, stealing, or destroying.

What to Do?

> I urge, then, first of all, that petitions, prayers, intercession and thanksgiving be made for all people—for kings and all those in authority, that we may live peaceful and quiet lives in all godliness and holiness. This is good, and pleases God our Savior, who wants all people to be saved and to come to a knowledge of the truth. (1 Tim 2:1–4)

There is a pattern in these verses that is rooted in the depths of the heart of Father God. We are to pray for political leaders *so that* we can live in peace, *so that* godliness and holiness may abound, *so that* our God will find pleasure, and *so that* all people will be saved.

That last sentence of this passage is immensely significant. It is one of the four glimpses of what Father God longs for and what brings him pleasure (as mentioned in chapter 5). God our Savior wants all people to be saved and come to a knowledge of the truth. He does not want anyone to be punished or to die without knowing him. And he does not want anyone to remain stuck in the knowledge of good and evil.

But it begins with prayers *for* all people, and especially political leaders. The Greek word translated here as *for* is the word *hyper*. It is a primary preposition which means over, above, beyond, on behalf of, for the sake of, etc. It is a very positive word. This is particularly significant when you consider that Paul wrote these words during the reign of the Roman Emperor Nero, a tyrannical ruler who persecuted Christians in particular. This is typical of Paul, who also wrote to the believers in Rome: "Bless those who persecute you; bless and do not curse."[15]

Among other things, Paul is saying that the road to peace begins with pouring blessing on people who do not deserve it. The call of the peacemaker is to bring evil rulers before the throne of Father God *with thanksgiving* and then intercede and petition Him for blessing to be poured out, so that their reign would become transformed by peace.

---

15. Rom 12:14

The Walk of the Child

This won't work if you approach it from a knowledge of good and evil perspective. You can't really bless and give thanks for a person whom you consider evil and deserving of punishment. And I question whether you can truly speak blessing over someone you hate.

One of the best role models we have of this kind of peacemaker is Daniel. Daniel was a young Jewish man when a foreign king named Nebuchadnezzar killed his family, destroyed his city, carried him off to a foreign land, and most likely made him a eunuch. The fruit of the Tree of Knowledge of Good and Evil would give Daniel every reason to hate this king and his people. But Daniel served this king and his successors faithfully and lovingly, even when their actions were evil. There is no doubt that Daniel prayed for peace and blessing with thanksgiving. And God frequently answered with supernatural demonstrations of his power and grace.

At the time of this writing, diplomatic relations between some nations are being stretched to the point where a shooting war could break out. Proud national leaders use inflammatory rhetoric and throw insults at one another. They portray the other country to be evil. They feel threatened by their opponent and could quickly find themselves thinking that it might be best to attack first in order to prevent an attack against themselves. This is not a good situation.

At the same time, there are voices among the church in the western world who speak in favor of doing battle or going to war with the evil forces in the world. This kind of holy war thinking is firmly rooted in the knowledge of good and evil, which (as we saw in chapter 3) is the corrupted wisdom of the devil. If 1 Tim 2:4 is true, then a holy war is the opposite of what lies on the Father's heart. And, as a peacemaker, I am troubled that such thinking finds room to spread in the church.

Although I know that my God can raise up good out of the ashes of any catastrophe, I truly do not believe that war can ever be the best path forward. Paul clearly states (in 1 Tim 2) that our prayers for political leaders which lead to peace will bring pleasure to our God.

You may be thinking: What do we do about an evil nation? Here's an example. My prayer for Kim Jong-un, the supreme leader of North Korea, is that he would have Nebuchadnezzar-like experiences. I pray that God would impact his life with supernatural demonstrations of power and goodness, so that the nation would experience peace, so that the gospel of salvation would find fertile soil in which to grow. And I pray that God would surround Kim with Daniel-like advisers. And my prayer for other national leaders, including the president of the United States, is quite similar.

> He will judge between the nations and will settle disputes for many peoples. They will beat their swords into plowshares and their spears into pruning hooks. Nation will not take up sword against nation, nor will they train for war anymore. (Isa 2:4, Mic 4:3)

8

Freedom from Violence and Criminality

> So Cain went out from the LORD's presence and lived in the land of Nod, east of Eden. Cain made love to his wife, and she became pregnant and gave birth to Enoch. Cain was then building a city, and he named it after his son Enoch.
>
> (GEN 4:16–17)

MOST OF THE VIOLENCE and crime in the world takes place in cities. The first city in the history of mankind was built by Cain, the first human murderer. And that heritage has a fundamental impact on every city built since that time. Consequently, cities in this world have a tendency towards violence.

And yet, God has prepared a city for those people of faith who long for a better Kingdom.[1] And in Revelation 21 we read that the Bride of the Lamb is a beautiful city.

One of the threads that can be traced through the Bible is the story of restoration, and in particular the restoration of the City. The enemy, the serpent from Genesis 3, planted a spirit of murder into the structure where many men and women dwell together in society. But Father God has been at work since the beginning to bring restoration and glory.

A powerful step toward restoration came with the establishment of Cities of Refuge when the descendants of Israel occupied their promised

---

1. See Heb 11:15–16

land.² These cities are a fascinating example of the foolishness of God being wiser than the wisdom of men: A key to the restoration of cities (whose foundation is under the influence of a spirit of violence) was to specify that these Cities of Refuge would be a place where murderers could experience safety, grace, and mercy! What an amazing God we have, who would think of that.

In Isaiah 61 we find the passage of scripture which Jesus read aloud one Sabbath day in a synagogue;³ that prophecy which describes Jesus' mission. Jesus was anointed to set a troubled people free from those things which oppressed them, after which that people would be released to renew ruined cities. This is a peacemaker calling.

Can a City Be Changed?

One of the most remarkable stories in recent years is found in the Mexican city, Cuidad Juarez, just across the river from El Paso, Texas. It was once a thriving city with open border crossings to the U.S. and a healthy economy. However, its proximity to the border made it an attractive place for the drug cartels. Violence increased to the point where the city became known as the murder capitol of the world. And then, in the space of just a few years, things changed dramatically.⁴ The murder rate dropped by about 90 percent and kidnappings ceased.

> Or again, how can anyone enter a strong man's house and carry off his possessions unless he first ties up the strong man? Then he can plunder his house. (Matt 12:29)

How could such an astonishing change happen so quickly? The secular media points to things such as more professional law enforcement, a reduction in corruption, and that the drug cartels have settled their differences. While all of these things may be true, they don't quite explain the rapid and dramatic change. A culture of corruption and a drug turf war don't just stop happening on their own. The underlying spirit of violence in the city would need to be bound before those things could be plundered.

---

2. See Num 35:6–15 and Deut 19:1–10

3. See Luke 4:18–21

4. For example, see Alexander, How Mexico's most dangerous city transformed itself, The Telegraph (Feb 17, 2016).

The Walk of the Child

Another part of the picture is a local pastor named Poncho Murguia. Poncho felt led of God to pray and fast for change in the city. And eventually, God opened doors and gave Poncho specific guidance in changing the spiritual climate of the city. I have heard Poncho speak about some of the things he has experienced during these dramatic years. There were especially two things he spoke about which stood out to me:

- God challenged him with a question: "Do you love this city?" Poncho realized that, even though he had been a successful pastor in the city for many years and he loved the people in his church, he didn't actually love the city or the people of the city. He needed to learn to love the city. Eventually he adopted the city, declaring it to no longer be an orphan.

- Poncho described that, for years, churches in the city had been holding meetings and praying, each congregation as if they were the only church in the city. But when congregations started coming together to seek God for change in the city, the spiritual climate started to change.

A Pattern for City Changing

> If you do away with the yoke of oppression, with the pointing of the finger and malicious talk, and if you spend yourselves on behalf of the hungry and satisfy the needs of the oppressed, then your light will rise in the darkness, and your night will become like the noonday. The Lord will guide you always; he will satisfy your needs in a sun-scorched land and will strengthen your frame. You will be like a well-watered garden, like a spring whose waters never fail. Your people will rebuild the ancient ruins and will raise up the age-old foundations; you will be called Repairer of Broken Walls, Restorer of Streets with Dwellings. (Isa 58:9b–12)

Deliverance from oppression restores a city. Eliminating violence and crime renews a city. Encompassing a city with safety is like repairing the walls of the city.

These verses from Isaiah 58 demonstrate a pattern for binding the underlying spirit of violence and thereby changing the spiritual climate of a city. It is a pattern based on the Principle of the Cross: not going into battle against the spirit of violence, but instead acting in the opposite spirit. Extending blessing and peace toward those who do not deserve it has enormous power to bind the spirit of violence.

Freedom from Violence and Criminality

This pattern is simple and straight-forward; almost like a mathematical equation. If you do x then it will bring about y. The first consequence of putting an end to oppression is that your light will become intensely bright. Or as Jesus put it:

> You are the light of the world. A city on a hill cannot be hidden ...
> In the same way, let your light shine before men that they may see your good deeds and praise your Father in Heaven. (Matt 5:14,16)

Jesus is speaking here about eliminating darkness. In the physical realm, darkness is the absence of light. Darkness is not in itself a quantity. You can't measure it or produce it. You can't "dark." A light can shine, but darkness can't "unshine." The same is true spiritually. Spiritual darkness is basically that state which arises when we who are light are not shining.[5] And one key to shining brightly is through delivering captives and eliminating oppression. This is what raises a city up from the depths, as it were, and sets it on a hill.

The business of restoration brings blessing on both those who are being restored and on the restorer: If you satisfy the needs of the oppressed ... the Lord will satisfy your needs. If you spend yourself on behalf of the hungry ... you will be like a spring whose waters never fail. If you do away with the yoke of oppression ... the Lord will strengthen your frame. Do you see the pattern here? When we use our resources to pour out blessing and bring restoration and freedom, then those resources increase!

Isaiah 58 and 61 demonstrate that the interests of our Lord are firmly planted in deliverance and restoration. He has given us a crown of beauty, the oil of gladness and a garment of praise. These are the things which are best suited to binding and plundering the spirit of violence.

Law Enforcement or Peacemaking

> No longer will violence be heard in your land, nor ruin or destruction within your borders, but you will call your walls Salvation and your gates Praise. (Isa 60:18)

Most communities in the world today are under the jurisdiction of one or more police forces, who are tasked with enforcing the laws of the land. In

---

5. You may be thinking, "What about demons?" Jesus' death on the Cross has completely defeated and disarmed the enemy. (See Col 2:15) So even though demons do exist, it is in the absence of spiritual light that they find room to operate.

North American English, the men and women of these forces are called law enforcement officers or peace officers, somewhat interchangeably. But these two terms actually describe fundamentally different things.

Law enforcement is rooted in the knowledge of good and evil. It is mostly concerned with ensuring that lawbreakers get their due punishment. Law enforcement frequently depends on a show of strength in order to force the lawbreaker into submission. With this mindset, the law enforcement officer needs to be armed both in order to protect himself and in order to outgun the criminals.

Peacemaking is primarily concerned with establishing and protecting a culture, so that its citizens may continue to live in peace. It is rooted in the Tree of Life, because the priority of the peacemaker is life and peace.

Let me give an example. A number of years ago in the city where I live, a film crew was doing a mock a bank robbery. They were in a bank's main downtown lobby at about closing time. However, the local police had not been informed about their film project. So when a passerby happened to see what appeared to be a man holding a machine gun inside of the bank and called the police, they prepared for action.

Norwegian police do not normally carry weapons. So when the call came in, they had to mobilize a force, hand out weapons and then send the force out to deal with the situation; all of which extends response time.[6]

The next day, my wife (who knew the police officer responsible for distributing the weapons) asked if the delay in getting an armed squad out onto the street was a problem. He answered that it really wasn't. As peace officers, they would rather avoid seeing a shootout develop downtown in the middle of rush hour. He was confident that, despite any delay, the robbers would eventually be caught—and much better if that took place out in the country where, most likely, no one would get hurt.

An officer with a law enforcement perspective would seldom think like that. When law enforcement is the priority, then it would seem far worse to risk letting the criminals get away than the possibility of innocent bystanders becoming casualties. In the end, a law enforcement perspective leads to a culture of violence. The knowledge of good and evil says that a lawbreaker has no value. And if a person has no value, then it really doesn't matter if they get wounded or killed. And if a potential lawbreaker looks

---

6. Once the police were on site, the misunderstanding was cleared up without any shots being fired. The film company was later fined for not having reported their activities in advance.

a lot like an actual lawbreaker, then the law enforcer can become quick to employ deadly force.

Unless you live in one of a small handful of nations,[7] you may find it almost inconceivable that the Norwegian police forces are normally unarmed. You might think that leaves them very unprotected. But the belief that a weapon will protect you is not a peacemaker thought.[8]

Some statistics. At the time of this writing, Norway has a population of about 5.4 million (about 1/60 of the U.S. population). A total of twelve Norwegian police officers have been killed in service since World War II.[9] (Only seven of these were firearm deaths.) Only five people have been killed by Norwegian police in the past eighteen years.[10] And yet, Norway is among the top twenty nations in the world for per capita rate of civilian gun ownership, with nearly twenty-nine guns per hundred inhabitants.[11]

By comparison, in the past decade approximately one thousand five hundred people per year have been killed by police officers in the United States;[12] while on average more than 160 American policemen have died in the line of duty each year.[13]

Why the huge difference? I believe that a major factor is the difference between law enforcement and peacemaking.

The Roots of Violence

Now, simply disarming or defunding the police forces of America is not a solution. Because the culture of violence and the culture of law enforcement need to change first. Changing a culture requires getting at the roots of the issue, and causing the light of the Kingdom to shine into those areas of spiritual darkness. And that can be uncomfortable, because the underlying

---

7. Iceland, Ireland, New Zealand, Norway and the UK.

8. The question of whether or not the Norwegian police should carry weapons has been up for debate several times through the years which I have lived in Norway. Interestingly, most police officers would prefer to remain unarmed.

9. Egeberg, "Ti politimenn drept," para 1. There have been an additional two deaths since that article was written in 2010.

10. Lindberg, "På 16 måneder," first 3 paras.

11. Wikipedia, "Small Arms Survey," Worldwide firearms table.

12. Wikipedia, "List of Killings," Historical data table.

13. NLEOMF, "Officer Deaths by Year."

The Walk of the Child

spirits (just like the serpent in the Garden of Eden) are very good at deceiving us to believe that they represent good and honorable things.

Jesus said that satan is a murderer from the beginning and the father of lies.[14] He is the root of all violence, and the source of that deception which leads us to believe that deadly force can be a good thing. As we saw when we looked at the Principle of the Cross, what lies at the root of this deception is the desire to conquer, the desire to forcefully succeed, the desire to win. In most cultures, we value success and celebrate those who win. And yet, such values are completely unlike the ways of Jesus.

Think about that. Jesus never forced anyone to do his will.[15] Instead, he said "If anyone forces you to go one mile, go with them two miles."[16] He frequently told people to "go and sin no more," but he also gave them the freedom to choose whether or not they would do so. And he never withdrew his love or his fellowship from people, regardless of how they behaved towards him. Those are very different behaviors from "going for the win."

So, in order to change a violent culture, you have to start by not wanting to win. And then that beam of spiritual light needs to shine into the culture. As in the case of pastor Poncho in Cuidad Juarez, a key turning point was the decision to love and adopt a seemingly unlovable city.

The Problem with Weapons

These next few paragraphs could well get me into trouble with some American conservative Christians. That is a risk I am willing to take, because we need to take a hard look at the deceptive roots of the spirit of violence.

A gun is a tool of violence.[17] If ever you point a gun at a person (or even threaten to do so) then you are violently forcing your will on that person. You may think that you have a right to protect yourself, or that your

---

14. See John 8:44

15. It could be argued that Jesus used force when he drove the businessmen out of the temple. But it could also be argued that he only used the whip to drive out the animals; and that "turning the tables" of the money changers was more a matter of shutting down business, than it was a display of rage. I wasn't there, so I don't know for sure. But I know that he only did what he saw Father doing. We'll look more closely at that incident in chapter 12.

16. Matt 5:41

17. I know that guns can be used for hunting. And though I am not a hunter, I am not opposed to hunting. That is not the issue here.

Freedom from Violence and Criminality

cause is sufficiently worthy to justify the use of force. But the use of force is *always* the opposite of the Principle of the Cross.

Now, take note. I have not said that gun ownership in America should be illegal. What I have said is this: if you consider using a weapon to threaten, harm, or kill another person, then you are operating in accordance with the spirit that wants to conquer and overpower. A peacemaker does not walk in accordance with that spirit.

If we really want to see the light of the Kingdom disperse the spiritual darkness which harbors the spirit of violence, then we need to be different from that darkened society—displaying Kingdom values rather than the values of men. Even when those human values may stem from cherished events in the history of our culture.

In the United States, one of those values is the right to bear arms, or the right to defend yourself. You don't have to search very far on the internet to find adamant biblical arguments supporting and justifying these rights. For the most part, these positions are rooted in the knowledge of good and evil. They cite the Law of Moses and the principles of punishment and justice.

I am not likely to win those kinds of debates, and I won't even try. For me, the question is: Do I want to be a peacemaker? If so, then I am called to lay down my rights and walk in the ways of the Principle of the Cross. I need to be eating from the Tree of Life so that I can see every situation with a heart of love, just as Father God does:

> But God demonstrates his own love for us in this: While we were still sinners, Christ died for us. (Rom 5:8)

At times, I am met with questions like: What would I do if someone threatened to kill me or my family members? I have never been in that situation, so I can't say for sure. I may try to restrain them, and I might get shot. Or I might see a miraculous turn of events by demonstrating the love of the Father. But I know that I wouldn't be carrying a gun (or any other weapon), so I wouldn't shoot them. I don't want to be in the position of sending someone to an eternal separation from God, just in order to postpone my own arrival in heaven.

That may seem foolish. But it's what Jesus did on the cross. He could have defended himself. But, instead, he reprimanded Peter for taking up the sword of defense. And it wasn't only Jesus. There is no evidence that Stephen, or any of the other martyrs whose stories are told in the book of Acts, exercised any right to defend themselves. Instead, they prayed for their persecutors and were willing to lay down their lives.[18]

There are those who claim that the only thing which can defeat a bad guy with a gun is a good guy with a gun. And there is a certain logic to such a claim. But it is not a Tree of Life perspective.

The Sovereign Lord said to the prophet Ezekiel that he takes no pleasure in the death of the wicked.[19] Take some time to think about that. The Lord God Almighty is revealing his heart here. Even though the wages of sin is death, he has no pleasure in the death of the wicked. By implication, the death of any person, whether wicked or otherwise, is displeasing to Father God. And he so wants for his children to have the same heart.

The idea that violence can be defeated by force is a deceptively ingenious scheme which the spirit of violence uses to strengthen its hold on a city. If we do not learn to see things from the perspective of Father God's heart, then we can easily be drawn into walking in agreement with the corrupted wisdom of the Tree of Knowledge of Good and Evil.

It has been said that the problem with spiritual darkness in a society is not so much the handful of very evil people in that society, as it is the overwhelming majority of people who are just a little bit bad.[20] The spirit of violence in your city will not be bound and dislodged as long as the majority of the church in the city believes that they are justified in using violence to protect themselves. Such strongholds can only be overcome by operating in the opposite spirit and in accordance with the Principle of the Cross.

The Cost of Winning

Wikipedia has a page with firearm-related death statistics.[21] There are some interesting things that can be extracted from those statistics. For example, sixteen of the top twenty nations on the list are in the Americas (about half of all North and South American nations)—ranging from four and a half to more than sixty-seven deaths per hundred thousand inhabitants per year.

Why the geographic imbalance? I suspect that it could be related to the legacy of the Conquistadors. In the sixteenth, seventeenth, and eighteenth

---

18. See also Matt 16:25, Phil 1:21 and Rev 12:11
19. See Ezek 18:23 and 33:11
20. My thanks to Arthur Burk, who first introduced this principle to me.
21. Wikipedia, "List of countries." These statistics cover the 74 nations for which data is available.

Freedom from Violence and Criminality

centuries, European explorers took advantage of their overwhelming firepower to conquer territories throughout the Americas. This would have opened the door for the spirit of violence to be established in the founding of these colonies. Many of these colonies violently rebelled in order to gain their independence, further strengthening the foothold of the spirit of violence.

The United States is no exception. Although the grievances of the American colonies against England and their king were serious, their Declaration of Independence was still an act of rebellion. And the ensuing war involved a lot of violence.

Many American Christians have been taught that America was founded by God-fearing men and that God blessed and supported the establishment of the United States. I don't disagree with that. I am thankful for the freedoms and godly principles on which my nation was founded. But it is wrong to assume that the blessing of God is the same thing as his approval. In my own life, I have experienced lots of blessing, favor and protection despite the fact that I have not always done what is right.

It is entirely possible, I might even say likely, that American pride in our War of Independence is a source of empowerment to the spirit of violence in America to this day. The widespread belief that crime can be subdued through a show of strength is a violation of the Principle of the Cross, and consequently a very different behavior than what Jesus saw his Father doing. This is the kind of issue that Jesus was referring to when he said, "What people value highly is detestable in God's sight."[22] The corrupted wisdom of mankind is not what God the Father wants to see displayed in the way his children behave.

> But I tell you, love your enemies and pray for those who persecute you, that you may be children of your Father in heaven. He causes his sun to rise on the evil and the good, and sends rain on the righteous and the unrighteous. (Matt 5:44-45)

What Jesus is saying here, is that the children should bear a family likeness to the Father. They are called to have the same heart. The Father loves his children—both those who are obedient and those who are not. It is his nature to bless and nurture people who do evil and who are unrighteous. And the peacemaker is called to share in that nature.

Father God wants his children to experience justice—in a framework of grace and mercy. So his way and his timing for bringing about justice is

---

22. Luke 16:15. See also Titus 3:1-2

very different from what human wisdom would expect. Jesus said that God will bring about justice, but at the same time questioned whether or not he would find a people of faith.[23] Do we actually trust God to dispense justice? Or do we feel a need to take the matter in our own hands? In the face of injustice, is it better to use force or take up arms? Or should we rather trust God to bring a justice that leads to true freedom, rather than a "freedom" under the influence of the spirit of violence.

For example, the initial history of Canada is similar to that of the United States. Both were settled by English colonists. But Canada did not gain their independence through a revolutionary war. According to Wikipedia,[24] the U. S. has more than five times the firearm death rate of Canada, even though Canada also has a high rate of gun ownership. One might expect the cultural similarity between those two nations to lead to similar rates of gun misuse. I attribute the difference to the influence that the spirit of violence has in U. S. culture.

The point here is that the U. S. appears to have paid a much higher price for their independence than most of us realize. It may well be that taking up arms in order to gain freedom has bought a "freedom" which is enslaved to violence.

The Power of Being a Peacemaker

I live in Bergen, the second largest city in Norway. Bergen is a city of about a quarter million people. There are no slums, and nothing like the inner city decay that might be found in larger cities.

Bergen is basically a safe city. I have never had reason to worry for my children who have grown up and walked to school in the midst of the city. But still, there is crime and there is violence. And much of that is related to alcohol. One aspect of the culture in Bergen is that, on weekends, people come from all over the region to take part in the night life downtown—mostly in the few blocks of bars and night clubs which the police sometimes refer to as "the wetlands."

For more than a quarter century, I have been active in an organization called the Night Ravens.[25] The basic concept of the Night Ravens is that when sober adults are present, bad stuff doesn't happen. Although the

---

23. See Luke 18:7–8
24. Wikipedia, "List of countries."
25. https://www.natteravneneibergen.no

Freedom from Violence and Criminality

Night Ravens is a secular organization, it's underlying premise is based on a biblical principle: that light disperses darkness.

We gather at about 9:30 pm. on Friday and Saturday evenings for coffee and a briefing, and then divide into groups of three or four people each. Usually we are two to four groups out walking the streets from about 10:00 pm until about 2:00 am (with a half hour break for a bite to eat). We wear bright yellow coats or reflective vests with the Night Ravens logo, in order to be visible.

And then we really don't do anything. We are not a militia or a self-appointed security force. We are not a bunch of big, strong, powerful men. In fact several of us are women in their sixties and seventies. We are not there to fix problems or to stop conflicts or to prevent crime; although that frequently happens. We simply observe. We carry phones and first aid gear, and if we come across something that needs attention we might need to call the police or an ambulance. But for the most part we just wander the streets of "the wetlands." And things don't happen.

Here's an example. Years ago, my group was walking along the central square. Across the square I observed a large man and his girlfriend having been stopped by a beggar. Some words were exchanged and the couple moved on. Perhaps the beggar said something unkind, because suddenly the man turned back and took several quick, threatening steps toward the beggar. Then he noticed us across the square, stopped in his tracks, turned around and went his way. That night, the beggar didn't get assaulted.

We have no way of knowing how often that kind of thing happens without us observing it. But we know that it does. And we are convinced that we make a significant contribution to our city being a safe city. By seemingly doing nothing!

Through the years, hundreds of people have told me that they feel safer because we are out on the streets—often accompanied by a half-sober hug and proclamations of how much they respect what we do. But in all of these years, I have only met with a handful of incidents: a few people who were so drunk that we weren't able to wake them, a drug overdose, a fight or two. That's not much.

In the first years, we were only out every other Friday night. After a couple of years we heard from the police that they could see from their statistics which nights we were out. There were fewer disturbances when the Night Ravens were on the streets.

The Walk of the Child

Why does this work? I believe it is because simply *being* a peacemaker has the power to bind the spirit of violence. We are not out to subdue crime and violence. We are simply out to be carriers of peace. And when peace is present, violence is inhibited. That fascinates me.

You don't necessarily need to start your own Night Ravens group to see a change in your city. But, like Pastor Poncho in Cuidad Juarez, you need to love even the unlovable aspects of your city. Ideally, the church in the city should come together in unity. But the momentum often starts with a seemingly insignificant group of believers who will commit themselves to being carriers of peace. As they seek the Lord *together* for wisdom to meet the violence in their city with love, goodness, generosity, and peace, the spirit of violence will be overcome.

> Live in harmony with one another. Do not be proud, but be willing to associate with people of low position. Do not be conceited. Do not repay anyone evil for evil. Be careful to do what is right in the eyes of everyone. If it is possible, as far as it depends on you, live at peace with everyone. Do not take revenge, my dear friends, but leave room for God's wrath, for it is written: "It is mine to avenge; I will repay," says the Lord. On the contrary: "If your enemy is hungry, feed him; if he is thirsty, give him something to drink. In doing this, you will heap burning coals on his head." Do not be overcome by evil, but overcome evil with good. (Rom 12:16–21)

Once again, this passage touches on blessing the wicked. The knowledge of good and evil would tell us that we can't bless the wicked. But both Jesus and Paul tell us that it is the nature of the Father to bless those who are evil.

We sometimes focus on blessing the wicked at "Bergen on Fire," a biweekly gathering for worship and prayer for the city. It is a very interesting exercise. At first I really struggled with the idea of praying something like, "Father God, I speak blessing over the human traffickers who control the beggars and prostitutes on our streets." But praying into this realm of blessing opens the door to a deeper revelation of the heart of God, our Father. And it changes the atmosphere of the city.

9

Economic Security

> Now the LORD God had planted a garden in the east, in Eden; and there he put the man he had formed. The LORD God made all kinds of trees grow out of the ground—trees that were pleasing to the eye and good for food.
>
> (GEN 2:8–9A)

MANKIND WAS CREATED TO live in abundance. The garden in Eden was a place of provision. There was no lack. It was an expression of an extravagant, creative and loving God giving of himself to his creation.

However, our experience of this provision was broken by the disconnection of disobedience. Instead of trusting God for provision, mankind took on responsibility for themselves. Eating of the forbidden fruit was a declaration of independence—a very costly one.

One of the consequences of eating from the Tree of Knowledge of Good and Evil was the experience of lack. When peace was broken, the land fell under a curse and ceased to be naturally productive. Instead, it was bent toward undesirable growth. From that time on, effort was required for the ground to provide food.

Most of us in the developed world today have very little experience with the hard work of cultivating the ground to produce food. Mankind has developed a wealth of technologies in order to produce more food with less effort than our ancestors with their hand tools could imagine. And so, rather than by the sweat of our brow, we simply exchange some coins or bills for food that is pleasing to eat.

And so we are deceived. We don't see the hard work. And we can easily be unaware of just how blessed we are. Although statistics may vary, there are still millions of people in the world today who are starving. And perhaps over half of the world's population have never experienced abundance.

Ed Silvoso, in his book *Transformation*, has laid out five pivotal paradigms for experiencing real and lasting change in a society. The fifth of these is:

> The premier social indicator that transformation has taken place is the elimination of systemic poverty.[1]

Put another way, poverty in a society is a result of the actions we take, both as individuals and collectively, in our efforts to provide for ourselves in a framework of the knowledge of good and evil. We create systems of trade, production, and distribution (or lack thereof) which are designed to give benefits to some at the expense of others; because we are greatly influenced by the deception that there is not enough to go around.

Silvoso's principle is that when a society is truly transformed by the culture of the Kingdom of Heaven (where there is no lack), then the practical consequence will be a society that has no lack. There may still be individuals who, through their own choices, experience some level of poverty. But the systems, traditions and behaviors which hold people in poverty regardless of their choices are eliminated as Kingdom values become widely adopted.

When we look through the lens of the knowledge of good and evil at the conditions of those who live in poverty, it is easy to conclude that the poor are largely at fault for their poverty due to their own bad choices. We might think that they should get a job. Or we might judge them for substance abuse or for immoral actions. We might even be tempted to look to scripture and think that they are merely reaping the consequences of what they (or their parents) have sown. That is not Kingdom thinking.

---

1. Silvoso, *Transformation*, 29

Economic Security

Transformation

> Do not conform to the pattern of this world, but be transformed by the renewing of your mind. Then you will be able to test and approve what God's will is—his good, pleasing and perfect will. (Rom 12:2)

For the peacemaker, the road to a transformed society begins with a transformed mind. We are called to abandon thought patterns rooted in the knowledge of good and evil, and rather be consumed by the Tree of Life. Then, our thinking and our actions will be framed by the nature of our Father, who causes his blessings to flow toward all people, regardless of their behavior.

The battle is in the mind—our own mind, and in the minds of the believers in our community. It involves tearing down arguments and pretensions that obscure Kingdom truth.[2] In the realm of economic security, there are two fundamental truths that need to become real in our hearts and minds:

- There is no lack. Father God is a good provider. There is enough for everyone, so it is not necessary to guard our own interests.
- It is the nature of the Father to bless his children, even when their actions don't deserve it. And that is meant to be the nature of his children as well.

The death of Jesus on the cross took away the certificate of debt that was against us, thereby putting an end to the curse. Where people live under a curse today, we who carry authority as sons and daughters of the King often bear some responsibility for having bound that curse[3] to them through our judgmental perspective.

OK. If these last few paragraphs leave you feeling condemned or burdened by the obligation to bring change to society, then you are missing the point. This is not about striving to make a change. Rather it is all about becoming a demonstration of the culture of the Kingdom—becoming an ambassador of the King.

---

2. See 2 Cor 10:4–5
3. See Matt 18:18

The Walk of the Child

Contentment

> All the days of the oppressed are wretched, but the cheerful heart has a continual feast. (Prov 15:15)

> All days are evil for the poor, but a contented person makes every day into a feast. (Author's translation from Norwegian Bible 2011)

I have chosen to translate this verse from Norwegian because there is a fundamental truth here which is a little bit difficult to see in the English translation. The core value here is contentment. A contented person is not looking for more (or less), but is inherently satisfied. A contented person may still have dreams or goals, but there is no demand and there is no dissatisfaction with the current status. A contented person does not experience lack.

Paul wrote specifically about contentment in connection with his own life and in connection with our attitude to wealth.[4] He wrote about being contented in every situation, whether hungry or living in plenty. And he wrote about how the desire for more was a trap; something Jesus called the deceitfulness of riches.

The writer to the Hebrews put it this way:

> Keep your lives free from the love of money and be content with what you have, because God has said, "Never will I leave you; never will I forsake you." (Heb 13:15)

The pivotal word in this verse is *because*. As sons and daughters of the King of the universe, we have every reason to be contented. But, in order to live a life of contentment we need to actually *trust* that Father God will never fail us. It is not enough to believe that the Bible says he will provide for us (and thereby hope it to be true). Trust is a very active thing.

There is a story which is frequently used to illustrate what it really means to trust. It is told that a tightrope walker had set up a tightrope across Niagara falls. After having walked across a couple of times, he asked the crowd if they believed he could walk across pushing a wheelbarrow. A man spoke up and said, "Yeah, come on. I believe you can do it." To which the tightrope walker replied, "OK. Get into the wheelbarrow."

That's where we find contentment. In the wheelbarrow, trusting Father God regardless of where he pushes it.

---

4. For example, see Phil 4:11–12 and 1 Tim 6:6–10

But most of us have a hard time bringing ourselves to get in the wheelbarrow, much less feel at peace there. And in most cases, what keeps us from that place is the orphan spirit.

The orphan spirit is one of the tragic consequences of eating from the Tree of Knowledge of Good and Evil. That fruit disconnected us from the Tree of Life and disconnected us from experiencing the love relationship between Father God and his children. Father God didn't become any less Father or God, he didn't change at all. But that disconnection has left us feeling abandoned.

The orphan spirit tells us that we are on our own, and therefore need to take care of ourselves. Every time we experience lack or disappointment, the orphan spirit whispers to us that we can't trust anyone else, and leads us to believe that the only way to get any satisfaction in this life is to grab it for ourselves.

These are pretty powerful lies, because they seem to have a certain logic behind them and because they often appear to be consistent with our experience. But they are lies. They totally misrepresent God's goodness, faithfulness, and provision. And they steal our peace and our freedom.

Walking in Freedom

I believe that the key to learning to walk in economic security is generosity. It doesn't help much if I just tell you to trust God and stop listening to the orphan spirit. Most of us will not manage to break out of those habits through sheer effort of will.

But the practice of generosity becomes a workshop in experiencing the provision and faithfulness of God. And that builds trust. And it can be a lot of fun.

When I was an unmarried engineer living in the oil-rich state of Alaska, I lived in a house connected to water, sewer, electricity, and telephone—services that weren't necessarily available in the homes or cabins where several of my friends lived. So they would come by to shower, fill their water jugs, make phone calls, do laundry, or whatever. One person even brought her dirty dishes to wash in my kitchen (she often washed mine as well, which was great!), because water is heavier than dishes. It was an interesting time. But there was no lack and there was a lot of trust going on.

After marrying and then moving to Norway, our cost of living and our tax burden about doubled, while our income shrank. Thankfully, the habits of an open and generous home are not easily shaken. There were times when the bank account ran empty, but there was still no lack.

On one occasion, my wife drove the car home from work followed by clouds of escaping steam. All of the symptoms pointed to a failed head gasket. Cars in Norway cost about three times what they cost in America, and we weren't in a position just then to buy another car. We weren't really in a position to have the head gasket fixed either.

The orphan spirit tried to get us to think that we would have to sell off some assets in order to have the money to fix the car. It threw us the lie that we couldn't pray for a miracle in this situation since we did technically have the resources to manage on our own. But we saw through that lie and prayed that God would fix the car for us. The next day there was no steam. We drove that car for more than a year with no problems. Not until the day after we signed a contract to buy another car, did the head gasket symptoms show themselves again.

I have to admit that most of my life has been blessed with ample resources. Though there have been occasional periods of apparent lack, the overall picture has been one of plenty or even abundance. I believe that to be a fruit of a contented, thankful, and generous lifestyle.

Which may leave you thinking: What about the contented, thankful, generous believers who do not live in abundance? What are they doing wrong? Does God play favorites? I don't have good answers to questions like that.

But we have a friend. A single mother who has lived below the poverty line for as long as we have known her. She has rarely experienced abundance. And yet I hardly know anyone who is a better example of trusting Father God as her provider.

She lives day by day, listening to the Holy Spirit step by step, and experiences his loving hand in the tiny details of daily life. For example, one weekend, the freezer compartment of her refrigerator started acting up. About then, an unexpected sum of money turned up—sufficient to purchase a new refrigerator. And so she tells me, "Oh, so that's why the Holy Spirit told me not to buy frozen goods for the weekend" (as she otherwise would have done).

Many of us might have been irritated or even blamed God for the refrigerator failure. But she saw the entire episode through the lens of thankfulness and contentment.

Stories like these build faith. But for that faith to grow, it must be planted in an environment of thankfulness and generosity. Where thankfulness is lacking, God's supernatural provision can easily be buried by our worries and our demands.

Practical Generosity

As I have previously mentioned, much of the Old Testament speaks within the framework of the knowledge of good and evil. Even so, it paints a picture of the heart of the Father (for those who have eyes to see). One aspect that comes clearly to focus is that the Father has a special place in his heart for the poor.[5] So we can learn a lot about what is dear to his heart by looking at what the bible says about the poor.

For example, farmers are instructed to be inefficient when harvesting their crops. They should leave some behind in the corners of their land, and pay no heed if some of the harvest gets overlooked. And they should welcome the poor to gather these leftovers from their fields.

And businessmen are instructed to not charge interest if ever they make a loan to a fellow citizen.

These are examples of practical generosity. But there is more. In both of these instructions, there is a promise that the Father will reveal himself as generous: Behave this way *so that* the blessing of the Lord may flow.[6]

The principle is very clear. Those who live lives of generosity open the door for the Father to bless them and all that they do, because in the economy of the Kingdom blessing has a way of snowballing. It is like a chain reaction. It multiplies itself. You can't out-bless God.

But there are still a couple of extremes to avoid:

- Being generous in order to manipulate God into blessing you is really a veiled form of greed, as well as a display of distrust. Father God is constantly pouring out his blessing toward you, so he doesn't need to be manipulated to do so.

- Feeling that you must give to others in order to be acceptable is not generosity. It is enslavement to some kind of rules-based living. There is no peace there.

---

5. In particular, three categories of poverty are frequently named together: widows, orphans and aliens (foreigners/immigrants).
6. See Deut 23:19–20 and 24:19–21

The Walk of the Child

The orphan spirit would like to push us into one or both of these errors, but we would do well to keep our eyes fixed on the goodness of Father God. True generosity contributes to repairing the disconnection brought about when mankind ate from the forbidden tree, and it disarms the orphan spirit.

As we learn to lead generous lives, we increasingly become an expression of the nature of our abundantly generous Father. And as his blessing is poured out on all that we do and everyone we touch, peace is increased and lives are changed. And for the contented person, every day becomes a feast!

10

Freedom from Lies, Deception and Accusation

> For the creation waits in eager expectation for the children of God to be revealed. For the creation was subjected to frustration, not by its own choice, but by the will of the one who subjected it, in hope that the creation itself will be liberated from its bondage to decay and brought into the freedom and glory of the children of God.
>
> (ROM 8:19–21)

WE ARE SURROUNDED BY lies. The so-called real world, the physical world which we experience with our natural senses, is but a shadow. Truth is a much richer experience.

Perhaps you have seen the 1999 movie, *The Matrix*. In a nutshell, this movie portrays a future where machines have taken over the world. But they need the energy from humans to keep themselves running. So they keep the humans enslaved by feeding their minds a virtual reality experience that has the people believing they are living lives of freedom, while they are actually enslaved as power generators for the ruling machines.

I suspect that the creators of that movie had no idea just how prophetic their story line is. The "prince of this world"[1] has so deceived much of mankind that they don't even realize they are enslaved to his rule. The fruit

---

1. See John 12:31, 14:30, and 16:11

of the Tree of Knowledge of Good and Evil, the curse over creation, and the disconnection from Father God all seem to be normal in this deceptive environment. Not unlike *The Matrix*, we live in a virtual reality which is a massive deception.

The prince of this world, as Jesus called him, is the devil or satan. The word devil is derived from the Greek word for slanderer, and satan is the Hebrew word for accuser or adversary. This adversary is untruth personified. Jesus called him the father of lies and said that lies are his native language.[2] He summed up by saying that there is no truth in him.

Deception

> Deceit is in the hearts of those who plot evil, but those who promote peace have joy. (Prov 12:20)

The big problem with lies is that they deceive us. A lie which we do not recognize as a lie is able to control us. We end up believing something which is not truth, and in so doing become captives to that untruth. This is deception.

The best lies are those which lie closest to the truth. Nobody is fooled by a hand-drawn dollar bill. But a carefully crafted counterfeit dollar bill may deceive many.

In the same manner, the father of lies has carefully crafted many deceptive realities which are very nearly true. And to the extent that those lies remain unexposed, we are ensnared and deceived by them—which leads to a life of bondage.

We have already seen examples of this in the previous chapter. Most of the world believes the lie that there are not enough resources, with the consequence that millions of people live in poverty. This lie seems to be true, because we experience lack and because we do not trust our Provider God. But the truth tells us that Father God is our Shepherd and we therefore lack nothing.[3]

We also touched on a huge lie in chapters 7 and 8: The lie that strength will secure peace. This lie is the opposite of the Principle of the Cross. It is founded upon the devil's nature and his rebellion. And yet, it seems so very logical and obvious to us that we can secure our peace through strength.

2. See John 8:44
3. See Ps 23:1

We are deceived to imagine that we can control our destiny and protect ourselves from enemies, either by the strength of our will or the strength of our hand.

Col 2:15 tells us that the enemy was completely defeated and disarmed when the certificate of debt that was against us got nailed to the cross. Think about that! It is not just that the devil will lose in the end. He is already completely defeated. And disarmed. He has no weapons, because they have been taken away.

And yet, we find that the enemy still has influence in this world. Why is that? It is because he is the father of lies. As long as a deceived person doesn't know that they are being deceived, they remain under the power of that deception. Even though completely disarmed, the enemy can still enslave us to the degree that we are in agreement with his lies. He is powerless, except when we give him power by believing something that is not true.

Strongholds

Before we go on, I want to clarify what I mean by a few terms. These terms are closely related, but confusion may arise without a clear understanding of how they differ.

Facts are pieces of information which are correct. Facts may be true, and yet still not represent Truth.

Reality is our perception of the facts. Our reality is framed by what we experience, and our experience is all too often distorted by the lies which deceive us.

Truth is the entire picture as Father God sees it. Truth is consistent with the nature and will of God, because Truth is a person.

Strongholds are ideas, beliefs, or concepts which we recognize as not being in line with truth, and yet facts and/or reality lead us to believe that they can not be changed.

> The weapons we fight with are not the weapons of the world. On the contrary, they have divine power to demolish strongholds. We demolish arguments and every pretension that sets itself up against the knowledge of God, and we take captive every thought to make it obedient to Christ. (2 Cor 10:4–5)

These verses tell us something very important about truth. As sons and daughters of the Living God, we are given weapons for a very specific purpose: to demolish strongholds. And those strongholds are the facts and realities which would stand in the way of coming to know Truth. In other words, we are equipped to expose lies and to bring Truth into focus. These are weapons that set people free.

Our weapons are for tearing down strongholds. They are *never* meant to be used for tearing down people. Even when faced with people who would adamantly force a lie upon us, we do not fight against flesh and blood. Walking in peace means always treating your opponents with honor and respect.

Identifying truth

> For the law was given through Moses; grace and truth came through Jesus Christ. (John 1:17)

When a lie is exposed, it loses its power. And Jesus said that, "you will know the truth, and the truth will set you free."[4] So the peacemaker will do well to train themselves in identifying truth.

In its most basic form, Jesus is Truth—just as he said. But that can be a little bit abstract when we are looking for practical guidelines for identifying truth. So it can be helpful to remember how Jesus described the father of lies, because those characteristics are exactly not truth. He is the enemy, the adversary, a murderer from the beginning, the father of lies, the accuser of the brethren, in whom there is no truth. This description can help us discern untruth from truth. A lie will:

- promote fear
- encourage shame
- feel like an accusation
- instill confusion rather than clarity
- quench faith or amplify doubt
- emphasize obedience over relationship
- discredit God

---

4. John 8:32

Freedom from Lies, Deception and Accusation

A statement or thought which carries any of these characteristics is not truth. It is a lie which needs to be exposed. Doing so will bring freedom, deliverance, and peace.

This bears repeating, because there are lies which we have perhaps believed for years or even for generations, that can be difficult for us to acknowledge as lies. Let's take a look at a few examples:

- *You are a sinner.* This is a total baldfaced lie. But there are many Christians who believe it to be true. Yes, I don't doubt that you have done something sinful during the course of your life. But that sinner is dead and you who trust in Jesus are a new creation.[5] Even though you may still occasionally sin, it is *not* your nature to sin. It is not your identity.

- *You are not good enough.* This is another total lie. God is love, and love is unconditional. There is nothing you can do which will lead God to love you more, or less, than he loves you now. He loves you because you are you. From a love perspective, it is totally irrelevant how good you are. He can not be disillusioned in you, because in him there are no illusions; there is only truth.

- *You must follow the rules.* The knowledge of good and evil leads us to believe that holiness is defined by our ability to follow the rules. Many may claim that we live by grace and are no longer under the Law; and yet live their lives (and judge others) by trying to meet the requirements of a sanctified lifestyle—which usually ends up being a set of rules for acceptable behavior in their particular Christian context. There is a huge lie here, which holds a multitude of Christians in bondage.

There are many more. The pursuit of truth is an activity of peace. It is good to examine things to see if they smell of fear, confusion, doubt or whatever. If they do then we can expose the lie and start digging for the truth. And the truth will always be found where there is faith, hope and love.

Peace is found in truth. Although we may at times need to be intentional about exposing lies, we do well to avoid being focused on the lies. A lie, once exposed, becomes a signpost to the Truth. For example, as we begin to see that there truly is no lack, our experience of Father God the Good Provider increases.

---

5. See Rom 6:1–11, Gal 2:20, and Col 2:9–12. We'll take a closer look at this in chapter 15.

The Walk of the Child

The Fleeting Thought

There is another pattern to be aware of when identifying truth. You have probably experienced this one many times. You get an idea, perhaps just a bit odd or crazy, and you think it might be something worth pursuing. And then, almost immediately, comes the thought that it wasn't such a good idea after all, but rather foolish or embarrassing or dangerous or whatever.

Often, what actually happens is something like this: The Holy Spirit whispers something to you; something fresh and creative and full of life. And then the father of lies (who can not himself create but only distort or imitate) tries to steal that fresh and creative word by turning it sour.

For example, you might suddenly think: "Maybe I should give John a call." Which quickly is followed up by something like: "No, he's probably busy." There is a good chance that the first thought was the Holy Spirit and the followup was not truth. Often you can expose the followup lie by asking if it was a distortion, if it instilled fear or doubt or shame, or if it felt like an accusation.

Accusation

> Like a fluttering sparrow or a darting swallow, an undeserved curse does not come to rest. (Prov 26:2)

Accusation is a particularly devious form of untruth because an accusation is based on facts. An accusation of something you haven't actually done will probably not hit home. But when accused of something for which you are actually guilty, the accusation might more easily find a place to land. So an accusation based on a fact may seem to be true. But it is not.

The key is the intent. The goal of an accusation is to demand a penalty for guilt. The fact of the guilt may be true, but it is only a partial truth. The complete truth includes the penalty for that guilt which has already been paid in full when the certificate of debt was nailed to the cross.

The accuser values righteousness only to the degree that punishment is required. The accuser wants to see the accused come under a curse. The accuser has no value for truth in itself, only for where facts can be used as a tool for destruction.

In this context, every accusation is not truth. Which means that anything that smells of accusation is a lie. Father God does not speak that way.

Freedom from Lies, Deception and Accusation

The Holy Spirit does not speak that way. And the peacemaker will do well to not speak that way.

When our Good Father speaks toward correction, he uses conviction to touch our heart. There is a huge difference between conviction and condemnation. Conviction softens the heart, so that it better sees from the Father's perspective; thereby drawing us closer to the Father. Condemnation feeds on the lie of our inadequacy, thereby bringing shame and separation. The intent of an accusation is condemnation, but the intent of conviction is restoration.

The Great Shift paid the penalty for all sin. There is therefore now no condemnation. But sin still has its consequences—which necessitate restoration. So when Father God puts his finger on something in our lives, he does so with words that bring life and foster restoration. He is Good, and everything he speaks works together for good.

> Whoever of you loves life and desires to see many good days, keep your tongue from evil and your lips from speaking lies. Turn from evil and do good; seek peace and pursue it. (Ps 34:12–14)

11

Freedom from Demonic Influences

IN THE PREVIOUS CHAPTER we saw that the enemy, the devil, is the father of lies and that lies can hold people in bondage. In this chapter we will look at some of the spiritual consequences of lies.

C. S. Lewis, in the preface to his book *The Screwtape Letters*, wrote that it is an error to not believe in the demonic realm; and an equally great error to give too much attention to that realm.[1] The spiritual realm is very real—I would say that it is actually more real than the so-called real world which we experience with our physical senses. Imagining that demons do not exist will not bring freedom from their influence.

So this chapter is not about chasing after demons. But it does acknowledge the reality and hopefully give some useful insight toward walking in peace and ministering freedom to the oppressed.

Mistakes, Habits, and Oppression

We may tend to think of sins as the things we do which are against the rules. We may tell a lie, or break the speed limit, or under-report our income on a tax return, or curse our neighbor or whatever. Or we might do something worse, like stealing from our employer or viewing porn.

If you are a Christian—if you have confessed Jesus as your Savior and Lord, and been crucified with Christ—then you are not a sinner. That sinner

---

1. Lewis, *Screwtape Letters*, ix

Freedom from Demonic Influences

was crucified with Christ; the old man buried in the waters of baptism. The sinner is dead and you are a new creation, raised up to newness of life.[2]

So what happens when you sin? First of all, let me be very clear: It is *not* OK. Sin is always bad. It is always destructive. But as a new creation, sin is not your identity. When you sin, it will typically fall into one of three categories: a mistake, a habit, or oppression.

If you accidentally break one of the rules, that is a mistake. We might not even call it sin, since it was not a willful choice to do something in rebellion or opposition to Father's heart. On the other hand, it might also be a symptom of how much yet remains to be learned about what brings pleasure to God our Father. Ideally, we learn from our mistakes and don't repeat them.

And then there are habits. These may be things we were in the habit of doing while we were yet sinners. Or they may be things we do in defiance. But they are repeat offenses. And we keep doing them as long as we do not train ourselves to stop. Even in this case, we are not sinners. We don't have a sin nature (which is dead), but we have sin habit (which needs to be unlearned). A sin habit is a very destructive thing, so we would do well to turn around and choose to break the habit.

But then there are the situations where we are unable to break the habit. That is demonic oppression.[3] We are face to face with a stronghold. When there are forces which hold us bound to a pattern of behavior from which we are unable to break free, there is nearly always a demonic influence at work.

There is a whole spectrum of demonic oppression, from somewhat trivial deception to overwhelming demonization. But every stronghold is rooted in lies. The tools for bringing freedom from demonic influence are the tools of peace—especially blessing and forgiveness.

Blessing

One evening, my wife and I were praying for a woman. Really, I should say that my wife was praying for her, and I was there for support. In fact, I wasn't necessarily paying a lot of attention at the moment.

Perhaps it is a consequence of a few too many rock concerts in my youth, but at times I find it a challenge to distinctly hear higher-pitched

---

2. See Rom 6:1–11, Gal 2:20, and Col 2:9–12
3. Note that I did *not* write demonic possession.

female voices. Especially if they tend to mumble, as this person did. So as they were digging into the details of a stronghold in her life, I was kind of fading out.

And, as I often do in such situations, I was defaulting to praying in tongues. My mind may not have been very fruitful, but my spirit was fruitful.[4]

Suddenly, a demon manifested. Now don't get the wrong picture here. There was no smoke or eerie presence or evil distortions. But the woman's voice changed somewhat, and spoke clearly and distinctly to me, "quit praying, Bruce."

My first thought was, "Was I praying? Well, I sure am now."

The demon, still speaking through the woman's voice, went on to try to entice me into conflict. I sensed that it was trying to get me to do battle with it, and (as I continued to pray) discerned that I should not let myself be drawn into that trap.

James wrote that when we resist the devil, he will flee.[5] Resisting is very different from attacking. A key facet of resisting is to not allow the enemy to dictate the terms of the confrontation.

So I continued to pray in tongues, not allowing myself to be pushed into fear or into conflict. I did not engage directly with the demon or allow it to drag me into a debate or argument.[6] My wife began to speak blessings over the woman. And after a few minutes, the woman said, "Oh, it's gone now!" No fight. No embarrassing manifestations.

When the demonic serves up aggression, we meet it with calm. In the face of lies we speak truth in love. When faced with accusation, we return blessing. In my experience, I have found three things which demons find very distasteful: worship, prayer in tongues, and blessing. And it seems to me as though speaking blessing in a firm, yet peaceful manner may be the most powerful weapon available to us for causing the demonic to turn tail and run.

---

4. See 1 Cor 14:14

5. Jas 4:7

6. There might be times where it is appropriate to interact with a demon, but this was not that kind of situation.

Freedom from Demonic Influences

The Prayer of Jabez

Hidden in the long lists of genealogies which make up the first several chapters of 1 Chronicles, is a most amazing prayer:

> Jabez cried out to the God of Israel, "Oh, that you would bless me and enlarge my territory! Let your hand be with me, and keep me from harm so that I will be free from pain." And God granted his request. (1 Chr 4:10)

At first glance, this could appear to be a very self-centered prayer. You could interpret it as, "Oh God, gimme, gimme, gimme." And yet, God granted his request. Undoubtedly, this is a prayer that touched the heart of the Father.

This prayer was also significant. The Bible tells us nothing about Jabez except that he was born in pain, and was therefore given a name that would remind him, and everyone around him, of pain. He probably found that to be oppressive. And so he prayed in a way that changed his life.

Looking closer, we can see that this prayer is a pattern for freedom from demonic oppression. Jabez touched on several things:

- *Bless me*: Cause my life to be wrapped in blessing. Make me a blessing. Fill the atmosphere around me with a fragrance of blessing.
- *Enlarge my territory*: Make me a pioneer. Enlarge my sphere of influence. Don't limit the blessing to myself or my family. Cause it to spread to my friends, neighbors, community, etc.
- *Let your hand be with me*: Teach me to walk hand in hand with you. I invite you to be involved in the daily workings of my life. Show me your ways. Teach me to think like you think.
- *Keep me from harm*: Expose the lies that influence my life. Show me your Truth. Remove any foothold which the oppressors may have, and give them no place within my expanding territory.
- *So that I will be free from pain*: I am not created for pain. I am not called to suffer damage at the hands of the enemy. Battle is not my destiny. I need only resist, the oppressor has no choice but to flee.

And God granted his request! Jabez asked for a bucket full, and God gave it to him without conditions or restrictions. That is the nature of our Good Father.

The Walk of the Child

Not long ago, the Lord reminded me of something. It was not uncommon on a summer day when our daughter was young, for her to come and ask me for an ice cream bar. She knew well that it wouldn't necessarily work to ask her mother (who tends to be a lot more sensible). But cuteness can be persuasive and I like ice cream, so the answer was usually yes.

After Father reminded me of that, he asked: "Do you think you are a better Father than I am?" The point is: Father God finds great pleasure in giving us what we ask for, especially when we come to him as children.

Note also that the prayer of Jabez is a prayer of peace. Jabez did not attack his situation or circumstances. He did not pray *against* anything. He prayed *for* blessing and favor. The result was freedom from the oppression.

A friend of our son frequently spent the weekend with us as they were growing up. This friend was plagued with food intolerance. There was only a fairly short list of things which he could eat. Everything else gave him trouble. Not surprisingly, he had a problematic relationship to food and was not particularly comfortable with mealtimes.

It would be wrong to say that he was demonized. But the situation was definitely oppressive and destructive. And so we set out to make mealtimes a blessing. We focused on peace and fellowship at the table. We were intent about there being an atmosphere of freedom. Over time, things began to change, and he started being able to eat more and more foods which previously had been taboo. Today, this young man is a cook! He is blessed, his territory is enlarged, and he walks in increasing freedom from pain.

Forgiveness

Often the entry point for a demonic oppression is some incident or offense which the oppressed person has experienced. It could be something as simple as a misunderstanding which felt traumatic or something as serious as physical, emotional, or sexual abuse.

Most people react to these kinds of things by setting up some kind of defense mechanism, in order to cope and perhaps prevent the pain from getting the upper hand. However, building these mechanisms on our own is a bit like clothing ourselves in fig leaves. They don't actually protect us. Instead they give demonic influences a foothold.[7] Often, our defense mechanisms become strongholds in their own right.

---

7. See Eph 4:27

Take fear for example. There are people who have lived so closely with fear that they feel unsafe without it. But fear is not your friend. Fear is a demonic oppression that wants to hold you in bondage. The same applies to things like shame, guilt, anger, and so on.

If you desire to begin walking down the path to freedom from demonic oppression, the Holy Spirit will be delighted to lead you. Ask him to show you the point of entry. He may remind you of, or show you a picture of, some incident that caused pain. You might even be surprised that the incident was more significant than you remember it to be.

Follow the Holy Spirit's lead. As he shows you how the pain has held you captive, give the situation to him. Most importantly, release the guilty person(s) from any claims of repayment or punishment which you may hold against them. If possible, speak out loud to declare your forgiveness.

Forgive from the heart. It is not enough to forgive because it is the right thing to do. (That would be a knowledge of good and evil kind of behavior.) Look at the person(s) who hurt you from a Tree of Life perspective. Ask the Holy Spirit to show you his love for them. And then rejoice in that love.

This breaks the foothold. The demonic influences which have seemed so deeply entrenched will lose their grip. Your territory will increase.

If you have been through deep or traumatic hurts during the course of your life or feel that you are unable to find a way out of the oppression, then ask an experienced counselor to walk with you through this process. Discovering footholds and painting them with forgiveness might just turn out to be something like a minefield, and then it is good to have someone walking with you who has been this way before. Those who themselves have overcome the oppressor, carry authority to help others walk into the same kind of freedom.

Overcoming

> For God was pleased to have all his fullness dwell in him, and through him to reconcile to himself all things, whether things on earth or things in heaven, by making peace through his blood, shed on the cross. (Col 1:19-20)

As we saw from the Principle of the Cross, true victory comes through foolishness, through weakness, and through apparent loss. And yet, the rewards of overcoming are full of freedom from oppression. That freedom comes not so much through our own efforts as through the shed blood of Christ. The victory is won, but there are yet more rewards to be claimed.

I can not emphasize this strongly enough. The path to overcoming passes through the fields of foolishness and weakness. We do not, we can not, overcome through our strength, our zeal, our wisdom, or our service. We overcome by the Blood of the Lamb, by speaking Truth, and by laying aside our self interest.[8] This kind of overcoming, foolish though it may seem, brings pleasure to Father God.

A quick look at the final verses of the seven letters to the seven churches (in Revelation) is in order here. Those who are victorious will be given:

- the right to eat from the Tree of Life (2:7)
- to not be hurt at all by the second death (2:11)
- some of the hidden manna (2:17)
- a white stone with a new name written on it (2:17)
- authority over the nations (2:26)
- to be dressed in white (3:5)
- their name always in the Book of Life (3:5)
- permanent presence as a pillar in the temple of God (3:12)
- the name of God, the name of his city, and the new name of the Son written upon them (3:12)
- the right to sit with Jesus on his throne (3:21)

All of these things are fruit of eating from the Tree of Life, walking in love, and wearing our true identity. We will take a closer look at true identity in chapter 15. But this reality is available to us now.

Peter wrote in his letter that our enemy, the devil, behaves like a roaring lion looking for someone to devour.[9] But he is the father of lies, and his lion-like behavior is a deception. The truth is that he was disarmed at the cross. That lion may make a lot of noise, but he is toothless. There is nothing to fear, because nothing can separate us from the wonderful, encompassing Love of Father God. Peace is ours.

---

8. See Rev 12:11
9. 1 Pet 5:8

12

Freedom from Conflict

IT WOULD SEEM THAT conflict is everywhere. Conflict arises where there is disagreement, opposition, or contention. And our experience probably tells us that it can not be avoided. In fact, I remember being taught in a creative writing class in school that the basic pattern for a story is to introduce the characters, build up a conflict, bring it to a climax, and then perhaps resolve it somehow. In other words, we seem to like conflict.

But conflict is *not* valued in the culture of the Kingdom of Heaven. James says that it is actually demonic.

> Who is wise and understanding among you? Let them show it by their good life, by deeds done in the humility that comes from wisdom. But if you harbor bitter envy and selfish ambition in your hearts, do not boast about it or deny the truth. Such "wisdom" does not come down from heaven but is earthly, unspiritual, demonic. For where you have envy and selfish ambition, there you find disorder and every evil practice. But the wisdom that comes from heaven is first of all pure; then peace-loving, considerate, submissive, full of mercy and good fruit, impartial and sincere. Peacemakers who sow in peace reap a harvest of righteousness. (Jas 3:13–18)

What James describes here is the fruit of The Two Trees. The corrupted "wisdom" of the serpent at the Tree of Knowledge of Good and Evil, which has infused the thinking of mankind, is the root of all conflict. And the wisdom of the Tree of Life is wrapped in peace.

Don't let the terms bitter envy or selfish ambition fool you. They encompass far more than we may like to think. It is too easy to read these verses and think: Well, I'm not *bitterly* envious or *selfishly* ambitious, so I'm probably OK. If so, you are only fooling yourself.

The term envy is translated from the Greek word *zēlos*, a word which in other contexts is translated as zeal. It implies passion, excitability and fervor. But it also implies provocation, indignation and jealousy. Zeal, if wrapped in love, can be favorable, but it can very easily become destructive. In the framework of good and evil, zeal will nearly always lead to conflict.

Selfish ambition is the NIV translation of the Greek word *eritheia*, which the King James Version translates as strife. The word implies taking sides, putting yourself forward, or making a distinction between people. At its worst, it shows itself as electioneering or intriguing for a position and using trickery to gain popularity. But it also encompasses any of the subtle behaviors we might use to bring about the result we desire in any situation.

I write these words with a bit of apprehension. For I am by no means immune to these things. There are situations where I find myself (usually far too late) adamantly pushing forward my position, arguing for things to go my way, or even manipulating circumstances toward my preference. It could be something as subtle as offering a particular serving to another person at the dining table (so that the bigger portion will be left for me). Or it could be a shouting match with a colleague. (Fortunately, the latter example is rare. But, unfortunately, I can't say that it has never happened.)

An Epistle of Straw

I find the letter written by James, the brother of Jesus, to be fascinating. Throughout history, many have looked upon it as inferior to other books of the Bible, and some have even questioned its inclusion in the Bible at all. Martin Luther called it "an epistle of straw." But it is really a matter of how you read it.

In the passage we just looked at, James writes that our wisdom is demonstrated through our actions. Now, if you read these words from a knowledge of good and evil perspective then you will probably conclude that you need to behave properly in order to gain wisdom. Which is exactly the kind of works-oriented instruction that does not mesh well with Luther's "by faith alone" revelation.

However, if it is read with a Tree of Life perspective, the message is quite different. I believe that James is actually saying something more like this: For those who are filled with the love of God, it is unnatural to live in conflict. Where love prevails, it produces the fruit of peace, consideration, mercy, and goodness. The one who loves is more concerned about the interests of others than about their own desires.

The distinction becomes more clear in the next few verses:

> What causes fights and quarrels among you? Don't they come from your desires that battle within you? You desire but do not have, so you kill. You covet but you cannot get what you want, so you quarrel and fight. You do not have because you do not ask God. When you ask, you do not receive, because you ask with wrong motives, that you may spend what you get on your pleasures. (Jas 4:1–3)

Conflict arises out of the orphan-spiritedness which is the heritage of eating the fruit of the Tree of Knowledge of Good and Evil. Our disconnection from Father God the Provider, our tendency to fend for ourselves, and the deception that there is not enough to go around, all lead us into conflict with those around us.

Yet, at the same time, James alludes to the truth that those who live in loving connection to the Father will receive the desires of their heart.

Why Not Rather Be Wronged?

> The very fact that you have lawsuits among you means you have been completely defeated already. Why not rather be wronged? Why not rather be cheated? (1 Cor 6:7)

For years I looked at this as one of the most challenging statements in the New Testament. But as I gain more insight into the nature of the Father's heart, this attitude is becoming more natural to me. Paul is not giving us instructions or commandments here, but rather expressing a fundamental aspect of the ways of Father God. In essence, he is saying: This new life in Christ is rooted and grounded in love; but the conflicts between you are a testimony to how much the knowledge of good and evil still has influence in your midst.

The Walk of the Child

For the peacemaker, the key to resolving conflict is found in the Principle of the Cross. For the foolishness of God is wiser than human wisdom.[1] Paul put it this way:

> In your relationships with one another, have the same mindset as Christ Jesus: Who, being in very nature God, did not consider equality with God something to be used to his own advantage; rather, he made himself nothing by taking the very nature of a servant, being made in human likeness. And being found in appearance as a man, he humbled himself by becoming obedient to death—even death on a cross! (Phil 2:5–8)

If the Creator of Heaven and Earth, the Lord of All, the King of Kings, made himself nothing in the face of conflict, who are we to stand up for our own rights? In essence, Paul says that we are called to wrap our interpersonal relationships in a clear understanding of our royal identity, while at the same time choosing not to exercise the rights accorded to that royal identity.

Once again, such a mindset can be particularly challenging for the American Christian. Most Americans are raised under the doctrine of inalienable rights.[2] Which also means that we value our rights rather highly. So the idea of laying down our rights and choosing not to win a conflict does not come easy.

And yet, the culture of the Kingdom of God invites us into its powerful foolishness. Peter put it this way:

> To this you were called, because Christ suffered for you, leaving you an example, that you should follow in his steps. "He committed no sin, and no deceit was found in his mouth." When they hurled their insults at him, he did not retaliate; when he suffered, he made no threats. Instead, he entrusted himself to him who judges justly. (1 Pet 2:21–23)

Peter highlights the key here. It all comes down to *trust*. If we really, truly and fully trust our Father God, then it is no problem to lay down our rights. Jesus and all creation long for us to be revealed as sons and daughters of our Father in Heaven.[3] And that revelation comes through trust. When we trust the working out of our daily lives to Father, we show ourselves to be his children. A chip off the old block, you might say. Few things bring

---

1. 1 Cor 1:25a
2. A concept which I do consider to be valid.
3. See Matt 5:45 and Rom 8:19

a father more pleasure than when their children resemble them, both in values and in behavior.

Love

God is love. The core of his nature is love. Everything he does, thinks and values is an expression of his core nature. It is all about love.

The Tree of Life is love. As we saw in chapter 3, the Tree of Life is an expression of Jesus, who is the exact representation of the nature of his Father. Everything that Jesus did when he walked among us was rooted in love.

So what does love look like?

> Love is patient, love is kind. It does not envy, it does not boast, it is not proud. It does not dishonor others, it is not self-seeking, it is not easily angered, it keeps no record of wrongs. (1 Cor 13:4–7)

A person who lives out these things *can not* be in conflict with anyone. Think about that! Love, as described here, *can not* be offended because Love always prefers the beloved.

Now, if Father God is love, then all of these things are true about him:

- he is patient and kind
- he does not envy or boast
- he is not proud
- he dishonors nobody
- he is not self-seeking
- he is not easily angered
- he keeps no record of wrongs

Our Father is not in conflict with any human, believer or not. This is the foundation of The Great Shift. Where there is no record of wrongs, there is no opportunity for conflict. Where patience, kindness, friendship, truth, honor and self control abound, conflict will dissipate.

You may be thinking: Wait a minute. What about evil people? Can God really not be in conflict with those who do evil? Being in conflict with the children he has created would make him inconsistent with his own word; he would not be love.

The Walk of the Child

The love of God is so encompassing that he can allow blessing even in the face of wrong choices. Like the father in the prodigal son story, he may be greatly saddened when his children choose the path of destruction. But our choices can not change the nature of Father God. He is still love, and he loves his children unconditionally.[4]

And he longs for his children to reflect his nature. A mature son or daughter of Father God walks in love and radiates peace. All of the things in the list above will show themselves to be true about the peacemaker. Not because the peacemaker is striving to achieve these behaviors. But because the peacemaker has allowed the love of God to be poured into their own heart to the point of overflow, so that they automatically live out goodness which is a reflection of the Father's nature.[5]

The distinction here is very important. Neither Peter nor Paul are telling us to act peaceful and loving in our own strength. Rather, they are describing their own experience of the love of God having been poured out into their own hearts and how that changed them from the inside.

This love of God is not a concept—you can't pour out a concept. It is a very real substance. God is love, and the Holy Spirit (who is intimately acquainted with the depths of God[6]) is an expression of that love. So it stands to follow that being *filled* with the Holy Spirit means there would be no place left in us for anything but the love of God. You can't make yourself loving on your own, because true love begins with God. You can only choose how much you allow yourself to be filled to overflowing.

The fruit of love (1 Cor 13:4-7) and the fruit of the Spirit (Gal 5:22-23) are very much the same thing, because the fruit comes from the love of God being poured out in our hearts.

Confrontation without Conflict

Being a peacemaker does not mean that we must accept everything and anything that people might do. Even when walking in love, we may still find ourselves interacting with people who do not behave in like manner. And

---

4. You may think that only those who are believers can be considered children of Father God. If so, I would disagree. I believe that all humans are created as his children. But they have been stolen by the enemy, and then redeemed back to their rightful Father through Jesus' death on the Cross. For example, see Eph 1:4-14.

5. See Rom 5:5 and Jas 3:13

6. See 1 Cor 2:9-12

love will at times lead us to confront unacceptable behavior. The challenge is to confront without creating conflict.

The key is love. We must first establish a right relationship with the person whose actions we wish to confront. That person needs to feel safe and to feel that they can trust us. Otherwise, we have no real authority to speak into their life.

The first and most important step in establishing a right relationship is forgiveness. If you have not forgiven a person, then it is impossible to confront that person in a manner which reflects the culture of the Kingdom of Heaven. If you are retaining the claim that the offender must in any way make restitution for whatever they may have done, then you are in conflict. Confrontation from that place will not result in peace.

As mentioned in the previous section, Father God is not in conflict with anyone. Which means that Jesus, who only does what he sees Father doing, is not in conflict with anyone either. There were times where he confronted people, but he did so without conflict.

A good example is his meeting with the Samaritan woman at the well.[7] Jesus knew about this woman's moral failures and how they contributed to destructive patterns in her own life. And he confronted them in an incredibly honoring manner. So much so that it became the woman's testimony: "He told me everything I ever did."

But there were more direct confrontations, especially with the Pharisees. Jesus said some pretty nasty things to them (such as calling them a brood of vipers), and many of them were offended. But he kept getting invited to dinner parties in Pharisee homes, so there must have been something about the way he confronted them which those who had ears to hear found attractive.

Cleansing the Temple

Perhaps the most extreme episode of Jesus in confrontation was when he drove the merchants out from the temple. I have met some people who use this story to justify their own angry and contentious behavior. So let's take a look at it from a perspective of love. All four Gospels describe the incident, but John's eyewitness account gives the most detail.

---

7. See John 4: 7–26

The Walk of the Child

> In the temple courts he found people selling cattle, sheep and doves, and others sitting at tables exchanging money. So he made a whip out of cords, and drove all from the temple courts, both sheep and cattle; he scattered the coins of the money changers and overturned their tables. To those who sold doves he said, "Get these out of here! Stop turning my Father's house into a market!" His disciples remembered that it is written: "Zeal for your house will consume me." (John 2: 14–17)

John says that Jesus was motivated by zeal for his Father's house, which is meant to be a house of prayer for all nations.[8] However, on his arrival there he found something more of a carnival atmosphere. And this was going on in an area which, according to the Law, was reserved only for the priests and Levites carrying out their prescribed activities of worship.

John describes Jesus overturning the bankers's tables and scattering their coins, commanding the dove merchants to take away their wares, and using a whip to drive the sheep and cattle out from the temple courts.

Clearly disruptive. But the gospel accounts do not state that he was violent toward any of the people present. So, was it conflict? What I find interesting is that it worked. The animals left, as did the merchants and moneylenders. They didn't fight back or have Jesus arrested—probably because they knew he was right and they were in the wrong.

It is also interesting to note that Jesus told the dove merchants to take the doves away. But he didn't throw the merchants themselves out. Which indicates that he did not withdraw his love and value for those people even while confronting them about their inappropriate activities.

Matthew tells us that what followed was a release of healing and childlike rejoicing in awe and wonder; which I would call an atmosphere of peace. But the temple authorities were indignant. I suspect it may have been because they saw no way to do anything about this uncomfortable situation without admitting guilt. They knew Jesus was right, but they didn't like it. So they resorted to nit-picking: "What authority do you have to do this?" and "Tell your disciples to behave reverently." But Jesus didn't let himself get drawn into an argument. He simply stated that the atmosphere of worship was unstoppable.

---

8. See Isa 56:7, quoted in Matt 21:13, Mark 11:17, and Luke 19:46

Freedom from Conflict

An Atmosphere of Worship

> When the LORD takes pleasure in anyone's way, he causes their enemies to make peace with them. (Prov 16:7)

A worshipful heart creates peace. A worshipful heart is a loving heart, a kind heart, an honoring heart, and a forgiving heart. A heart leaning in this direction brings pleasure to the Father, which causes peace to abound. In the same manner that light disseminates darkness, a worshipful heart radiates peace and routs the spirits of strife, anger, and conflict.

In this context, worship is far more than singing songs of praise. Worship encompasses all of the ways that we can express the love of God which has been poured out in our hearts; not conformed to the ways of this world, but living a transformed lifestyle.[9]

In several of his letters, Paul encouraged us to live at peace with everyone.[10] He was especially specific in his letters to Timothy that the fruit of a pure heart would be love rather than contention and kindness rather than quarreling. I would conclude that it is not possible to communicate the truth of the gospel if the message is not delivered in an atmosphere of worship.

In the atmosphere of worship, there is no room for arguments, for quarreling, for anger, for disrespect, or for dishonor. The challenge, then, is to carry an atmosphere of worship in the face of opposition or degradation.

To the degree that you are living in the experience of being truly loved, you will not be offended. For love can not be offended. To the degree that you are walking in love, you will not need to win or even to be understood. A mature son or daughter of God has nothing to fear from insults or accusations which may be directed at them, because an undeserved curse does not come to rest.[11] We who carry an atmosphere of worship have the power to end any conflict by acting in love, which covers over a multitude of sins.[12]

---

9. See Rom 12:1–2
10. See, for example, Rom 12:18, 2 Cor 13:11, Eph 4:3, Col 3:15, 1 Tim 1:3–7, and 2 Tim 2:16 and 2:23–25
11. Prov 26:2
12. See Jas 5:20 and 1 Pet 4:8

13

Freedom from Worry

AT THE CLOSE OF chapter 2, I told the story of an airplane accident. Although that was an unusually dramatic event, it was not the only potentially frightening incident I have experienced through my many years.

Like the time I was sitting in a car in the midst of a traffic jam in an African city. It seemed as though the whole city was in gridlock. We had hardly moved for about an hour, after traffic had been disrupted by the passing of a presidential motorcade. And then we heard gunfire. I didn't think very much of it at first, until I noticed that everyone else in the car had thrown themselves to the floor of the vehicle at the first popping sounds. And there I was, happily (and perhaps naively) looking out the windows, wondering what was going on.

Fear Is Not Your Friend

I guess that I am not very good at fear. And I have come to understand that to be a good thing. It may seem a bit naive or perhaps foolish. But I live as though those things which are out of my control are going to work out without my help. It's a childlike perspective.

It hasn't always been that way. But the more I have come to know and trust Father God, the more he has set me free from worry and fear. It has a lot to do with what you choose to look at. Or, as the psalmist put it: "I lift up my eyes to the mountains—where does my help come from? My help comes from the LORD, the Maker of heaven and earth."[1]

Fear[2] is not a rational thing, it is an evil spirit. Fear has a way of making itself feel comforting, but fear is *not* your friend. Not ever.

> There is no fear in love. But perfect love drives out fear, because fear has to do with punishment. The one who fears is not made perfect in love. We love because he first loved us. (1 John 4:18–19)

There are two main points I would like to highlight from these verses:

- Fear and love are kind of like oil and water. They don't belong together. They displace each other. If you are filled with love, then there is no place for fear. Giving Father room to fill you with his love will drive out all of the fear.
- Fear has to do with punishment. But, after The Great Shift, there is truly nothing left to punish. So fear is based on a lie. The Truth is found in Love.

That may seem like a nice theory. But how do you make it work in practice? Especially if you are one of the many people in this world whose life is influenced by fear.

I believe a lot can be gleaned from the surrounding verses in 1 John 4. The passage is about love. The source of that love is God, who is love, and who fills us with his love, and who lives in us. And all of that love will drive out all of the fear. But it really helps to look the right direction.

In fact, you might find it helpful to take a break right now and meditate on that chapter.

Meditation

Meditation is simply thinking or reflecting about something over a period of time. Another word for it is contemplation. And so, most of us are actually pretty good at meditation—by looking from various angles at what could go wrong and how that might affect us. That kind of meditation is called worry. But worry is really nothing more than meditating on a lie.

---

1. Ps 121:1–2
2. I am not referring to the fear of the Lord here. That is an entirely different thing, which is outside the scope of this chapter. The fear of the Lord *does not* produce worry.

The Walk of the Child

Paul, in his letter to the Philippians encourages us to live a life full of joy. He said it rather strongly, and even repeated himself: "Rejoice in the Lord always. I will say it again: Rejoice!" And then he followed up by admonishing us to not worry.

> Be anxious for nothing, but in everything by prayer and supplication with thanksgiving let your requests be made known to God. And the peace of God, which surpasses all comprehension, shall guard your hearts and your minds in Christ Jesus. Finally, brethren, whatever is true, whatever is honorable, whatever is right, whatever is pure, whatever is lovely, whatever is of good repute, if there is any excellence and if anything worthy of praise, let your mind dwell on these things. (Phil 4:6–8 NASB)

Let your mind dwell on these things! This is not just the antidote to worry, but the key to living a lifestyle unfettered by worry.

Simply put, Paul is saying that in order to live a life of joy, we need to put aside our misdirected meditation (worries) about what could go wrong and instead meditate on God's goodness.

The orphan spirit would like to convince us otherwise. It would direct our attention to the things which are out of our control, the things that could possibly go wrong, the things that we might not have the resources to deal with, or the potential for loss of even those resources which we feel that we do have. Fear and anxiety are two of its most effective tools for keeping people in bondage.

There are a number of things we can do to break out of orphan-spirited practices. And they pretty much all involve letting our minds dwell on the good and right and excellent things, rather than the deceptive warped perspectives served to us by fear and anxiety.

For example, the insurance industry is built upon exploiting our fears.[3] They play upon our fears in order to sell us products which give us the illusion that we can control the things that are outside of our control. They market themselves with ideas like giving us the stability of a rock, or being our comforter or our provider or our safety net. And if the orphan spirit gets its way then we might just find ourselves subscribing to a low quality substitute for everything that Father God has said he would be for us.

---

3. I am *not* saying that is is wrong to buy insurance. In fact, I strongly encourage you to have the insurance which the law requires or which is necessary for your contracts or obligations. The point here is to not be under the influence of fear.

Another example is how we go about structuring our relationships. Most organizations, be they businesses or churches, or whatever, have a hierarchical structure and a set of statutes or by-laws. Frequently, the hierarchy and the rules are shaped by the potential for things going wrong or the fear that someone might misuse their authority or take advantage of the system. Even though it is good to prevent such things from happening, it is not good for a relational structure to be built on a framework of fear.

How many of your decisions in a day are based on fear? Do you choose your clothing from a fear of what others may say about your wardrobe? Do you avoid eating certain foods in fear of how they might affect your health? Please don't misunderstand me here. It is not wrong to dress well or to eat healthy. The question here is to what degree are our choices driven by fear?

And to what degree might fear have influenced your salvation? Many people in my generation came to faith through fear. "If Jesus were to come again this night, where would *you* be?" For years, my wife found it difficult to build an intimate relationship with Father God, largely due to the influence that fear had in how she came to faith. Fear hinders intimacy. But perfect love casts out fear.

Trust

In essence, it all boils down to trust. Do we really, and I mean *really*, trust God to be our Good Father? Can we say, like Shadrach, Meshach and Abednego, that we trust our God, even if he *might not* save us from impending peril?[4] Peace is not so much about bad stuff not happening as it is about being secure regardless of the circumstances. Peace is being able to trust, even when the airplane on which you sit is hurtling toward an unknown fate.

Peter wrote something very significant about trusting:

> Therefore humble yourselves under the mighty hand of God, that
> He may exalt you at the proper time, casting all your anxiety on
> Him, because He cares for you. (1 Pet 5:6–7)

One thing Peter is saying here, is that the act of turning over your worries to Father God is an expression of humility. In so doing, you are placing your trust in Father and acknowledging his provision and compassion. This is worship in Spirit and in truth.

---

4. See Dan 3:17–18

The Walk of the Child

Most of the places where you find the word "faith" in the New Testament, it could be substituted with "trust." Because true faith is much more than an intellectual acknowledgment of something being correct. Faith is confidence in what we hope for and assurance about what we do not see.[5] In other words, faith involves trusting Father God because of who he is, even when all of the evidence appears to be saying otherwise.

I often say that the opposite of faith is control. Because trusting involves releasing control, casting away your anxieties, and expecting goodness and mercy.

Which brings us back to Philippians 4:6–8. Thankfully turning your anxieties over to the One who does not worry, fills both your heart and your mind with peace beyond comprehension. When that peace is established in the core of your being, then the external events of life are unable to touch you. You may not get there in one step, but the practice of dwelling on those things good, honorable, right, pure, excellent, and praiseworthy is like fertilizer to the soul. It stimulates the roots of trust to go deep and invites the peace which overcomes the world to find a dwelling place in your heart.

On the evening just before Jesus was arrested, he ate the Passover meal together with his disciples. John gives an eyewitness account of that dinner party in chapters 13–16 of his gospel. It was an evening filled with Jesus' words of encouragement to his followers. He wrapped up the evening by saying:

> I have told you these things, so that in me you may have peace. In this world you will have trouble. But take heart! I have overcome the world. (John 16:33)

It is a very significant statement. The world may throw it's stuff at you, but that stuff is defeated. Instead, Jesus is calling us to be filled with peace. And he told his disciples things that would establish in them a peace which the troubles of the world can not touch.

There is much to be gained from letting your mind dwell on the things which Jesus said in John 13–16. The passage is soaked in peace. Not all of the things that Jesus said and did in those four chapters make sense to the mind, because Jesus is speaking to hearts and spirits. But he said those things so that we would have peace. And his word never returns void.

---

5. Heb 11:1

14

A Haven of Blessing and Rest

> It's useless to rise early and go to bed late, and work your worried fingers to the bone. Don't you know he enjoys giving rest to those he loves?
>
> (PS 127:2 THE MESSAGE)

THE PLACE OF PEACE is a haven of blessing and rest. In the place where nothing can touch us, where there is no fear, where blessing abounds—there is rest.

A Man after My Own Heart

Father God called King David "a man after my own heart."[1] That is actually a pretty astonishing testimony.

If you look at the life of David from a knowledge of good and evil perspective, he actually comes up fairly short. There was the incident with Bathsheba and the ensuing cover-up which led to the murder of her husband. There was the time David ordered a census and brought guilt upon the nation. He was disqualified from building the Temple because of all the bloodshed he had committed as a man of war. And there were other things as well.

---

1. See Acts 13:22 and 1 Kgs 15:3

The Walk of the Child

So what was it about David? We might easily interpret the phrase "a man after my own heart" to mean something like: A man who follows my ways and who does what pleases me. But I rather think that it means something more like: A man who desires to know my ways, whose desire is to know what lies on my heart.

Many of the psalms written by David are expressions of his emotional ups and downs. But his emotions are also anchored in his ongoing experience of Father God's love. This anchor is perhaps most clearly expressed in Psalm 23, so let's take a closer look.

> The LORD is my shepherd, I lack nothing. He makes me lie down in green pastures, he leads me beside quiet waters, he refreshes my soul. He guides me along the right paths for his name's sake. Even though I walk through the darkest valley, I will fear no evil, for you are with me; your rod and your staff, they comfort me. You prepare a table before me in the presence of my enemies. You anoint my head with oil; my cup overflows. Surely your goodness and love will follow me all the days of my life, and I will dwell in the house of the LORD forever. (Ps 23:1–6)

David begins with a revelatory proclamation: Father God watches over me and provides for all of my needs. There is no lack. Even when I might feel as though I experience lack, that apparent reality is not the truth. I may not see the provision, but I know that Father is in control, so I don't need to be.

When I am burdened by obligations, expectations, stress or whatever, he is thinking rest. And he abundantly pours out his rest over me. The love of the Father stretches me out on the delightful grassy banks of a quiet stream, and brings times of refreshing to my inner being. Whatever turmoil may surround me can not touch me in this place of rest.

When I am feeling lost, he wants to play Follow the Leader. He calls me his child. I am his and I carry his name. He leads me in paths of safety and blessing, and I am invited to follow his footsteps. In this way, his child bears his likeness.

We walk hand in hand. It really doesn't matter where we go because he is with me. It could even be the darkest and most evil surroundings imaginable. I am comforted by his authority and his majesty. His overwhelming goodness assures me that nothing can bring us harm.

A Haven of Blessing and Rest

When I might be anticipating a potential fight, he is thinking picnic. Instead of facing a battle, I find myself at the spa. He is so at rest that I can hardly cope. It's just overwhelming.

In light of all of this, it becomes increasingly clear: goodness and love are deliberately pursuing me. Blessing is my birthright and I am swimming in it. I have found my home and it is truly a restful haven.

OK. I've taken some liberties in my interpretation of the psalm. But I do hope you can see what I am aiming at. Peace is found in the center of the love of the Father. It is not found in fixing our external circumstances, but rather in the safety of his gaze regardless of the circumstances.

David understood this. He was a man after God's own heart. He could occasionally lose sight of the peace, but he knew whom to look to when that happened. One example:

> Then I called upon the name of the Lord: "O Lord, I beseech You, save my life!" Gracious is the Lord, and righteous; yes, our God is compassionate. The Lord preserves the simple; I was brought low, and He saved me. Return to your rest, O my soul, for the Lord has dealt bountifully with you. For You have rescued my soul from death, my eyes from tears, my feet from stumbling. I shall walk before the Lord In the land of the living. I believed when I said, "I am greatly afflicted." I said in my alarm, "All men are liars." (Ps 116:4–11)

What David is describing here is how he briefly lost peace, and then recovered it. It began when he believed the lie that he was afflicted. That opened the door for fear, which led to paranoia. But when he turned his focus away from the circumstances and instead set his gaze on Father God, everything changed. Then he could say to himself: Now you can find rest again.

> The LORD bless you and keep you; the LORD make his face shine on you and be gracious to you; the LORD turn his face toward you and give you peace. (Num 6:24–26)

The Aaronic priestly blessing is a blessing of rest. The face of the Lord is his favor and his Spirit. In the light of his face there is nothing to fear. There we can rest.

The Walk of the Child

The Playground

Mankind was created for rest. When Father created Adam and Eve, he placed them in the Garden. It was a place of abundant provision, continuous rest, and joyful delight. Adam and Eve were not placed in the garden as gardeners—no human effort was needed for the trees to produce fruit that was pleasing to the eye and good to eat. In fact, I believe that Father's intent is for this world to be our playground.

This idea of a playground may surprise or perhaps even shock you. But I find a good basis for it in Proverbs 8. The chapter starts out with a person called Wisdom inviting any who would hear to learn from her (verses 1–21). Although this person is at first described as being of female gender, Wisdom begins to describe its origin in a manner which is undoubtedly that of the only begotten Son of the Father (verses 22–29). And then, Wisdom makes a most amazing statement:

> Then I was at his side each day, his darling and delight, playing in his presence continually, playing on the earth, when he had finished it, while my delight was in mankind. (Prov 8:30–31 NEB)

Now, it may well be that your favorite translation uses something like the verb rejoicing rather than the verb playing, as used by the New English Bible. But playing is a more accurate translation of the Hebrew word *sachaq*. In this verse, most translations in the German tradition (including nearly all Norwegian translations) use playing, as did Wycliffe (the late fourteenth century translator to English). However, most translations in the English tradition (whose roots are in sixteenth-century Calvinist scholarship) have chosen to translate it as the more respectable behavior of rejoicing.

I might also mention that, while faithfully translating the verb as playing, the NEB translation leaves out an important noun. The NASB translates the first phrase of verse 30 as "Then I was beside him, as a master workman." The Hebrew word *'amown* used here means craftsman, skilled workman, artisan or similar.

Pulling both of these two facets into view from their obscurity, we get a picture of the Son of God (by whom and through whom all things were created) joyfully and playfully running about the earth making and delighting in things of beauty. It was his playground. It was here he placed Adam and Eve, in whom he was delighted.

A Haven of Blessing and Rest

However, when Adam and Eve ate the fruit of the Tree of Knowledge of Good and Evil, everything changed. The land came under a curse, the abundant provision was broken and rest became a fleeting thing.

When the culture of the Kingdom of Heaven flows in a society, the curse on the land gets pushed back. The Transformation videos, produced in the 1990s by George Otis Jr, document several cases (such as in Fiji and in Almolongo, Guatemala) where changes in the spiritual climate led to healing of the land. And healing of the land brings rest.

This kind of healing was an underlying goal when Father God led a people of his choosing out of Egypt and into the Promised Land. The promise was a land flowing with milk and honey, a land where they could enter rest.

But first it would be necessary to displace the nations who inhabited the land. These were seven people groups who, through their practices, had contributed greatly to the curse upon the land. The curse was so sickening that the land itself "vomited them out."[2]

The calling on the people of Israel was to inhabit the land in a way that pushed back the curse, thereby revealing once again the place of rest—the playground. The potential in the land is huge. For example:

> For the LORD your God is bringing you into a good land—a land with brooks, streams, and deep springs gushing out into the valleys and hills; a land with wheat and barley, vines and fig trees, pomegranates, olive oil and honey; a land where bread will not be scarce and you will lack nothing; a land where the rocks are iron and you can dig copper out of the hills. (Deut 8:7–9)

He says that it is a lush land, with plenty of water, a land where good food is abundant and a land with minerals. The mention of iron and copper is significant—because, unlike water or food, these minerals have no practical value unless they are made into something. So, in essence, what Father is saying here is that he is not just providing the basic needs of food and drink, but also allowing for expressions of creativity.

When my granddaughter was two years old, one of the things that she did when visiting our home was to go into the office and find a piece of paper on which to draw. Like iron in the rocks and copper in the hills, I am delighted to make sure that there is paper available for her to find. At that age, her scribblings were really not much to look at. But she's our grandchild, so her drawings would still end up on the refrigerator door.

---

2. See Lev 18:24–28, Lev 20:22–24, and especially Deut 9:3–6

The playground is an environment where we are free to explore our creativity. What we do or make doesn't have to be useful—that is not the purpose of play. Even when we think we might be doing great things, it could well be that Father is no more interested than to hang them on his fridge, because he doesn't need our service, but he most certainly finds pleasure in our play. We were created to dwell in this place of rest.

Being a Blessing

The Lord God's promise to Abram was that he would be so blessed that all peoples would be blessed through him.[3] That is a pretty huge promise. And the promise applies to all his offspring, which includes us who are of the family of faith.[4] So the calling to be a blessing rests on us today. A son or daughter of Father God is a blessing to those around them, through the peace and rest they carry.

> But I say to you, love your enemies and pray for those who persecute you, so that you may show yourselves to be sons of your Father who is in heaven; for He causes His sun to rise on the evil and the good, and sends rain on the righteous and the unrighteous. (Matt 5:44-45 NASB with footnote)

As previously mentioned, it is the nature of Father God to bless—regardless of whether or not we think their behavior might deserve it. And we are revealed to be his children as we live out that same nature.

You can't do this in your own strength or through your own effort. But it will become more and more your nature as you learn to trust Father and rest in that trust.

God's promise to Abram was: I will bless you, you will be a blessing, and all peoples will be blessed through you. God is the initiator of the blessing. He did not lay on Abram any responsibility for the peoples of the world being blessed. Rather, he said that the overflow of the blessing on Abram would leak out onto everyone around him.

That is the calling that rests upon the people of the faith of Abraham. Just like David, the man after God's own heart, sang in Psalm 23. We increasingly become a haven of blessing and rest.

---

3. See Gen 12:1-3
4. See Rom 4:16

A Haven of Blessing and Rest

In peace I will lie down and sleep, for you alone, LORD, make me dwell in safety. (Ps 4:8)

15

True Identity

THE APOSTLE JOHN, IN chapter 13 of his eyewitness account of the life of Jesus, tells us the story of the time Jesus washed the feet of his disciples. As an introduction to the story, John makes an interesting observation: Jesus knew who he was, where he came from, and where he was going.[1] In other words, Jesus washed his disciples's feet from a conscious and intentional experience of his own true identity. Because he *knew* with all of his being that he was the beloved Son of Father God, he wrapped himself in a towel and took on the role of a menial servant.

Allow me to reiterate. Jesus completely grasped his true identity. He knew who he was, so he didn't need to prove anything. He could appear to be the most lowly of servants without feeling any threat to his value or to his sense of well being. That is a place of peace and freedom

Who Are You?

You are beloved! You, specifically you, were created because Father God loves you and enjoys you and delights to fellowship with you. This is true of every person, whether believer or not. This is the foundation of identity. Every person is inherently valuable.

But there is more. You are unique. You are desired. There is something planted in you which is not found in any other person. There is something

---

1. See John 13:1–3

True Identity

in the heart of God which can only find its fulfillment in Father God's relationship to you and only you.

I have mentioned this in previous chapters, but it is worth repeating: You are not a sinner. Sin is not your identity. It may have been your habit (and it might to some extent still be) but it is not what you are created to be.

Neither is your identity your accomplishments or your failures. Your identity is not what you do or what you have done. Your dreams and your preferences may be a hint at the uniqueness of your identity, but your true identity is not defined by such things.

True identity is found in relationship: Our relationship to Father God and our relationships with those around us.

> If it is possible, as far as it depends on you, live at peace with everyone. (Rom 12:18)

Your identity is not defined by how others relate to you. Rather, when you walk in your true identity, you will radiate a peace which influences all of your relationships.

Body Parts

A few years ago I was asked to lead a small missions team from a local bible school. The team had already been together for a week and a half in Germany before meeting me in Scotland for the second half of their outreach.

I was at a disadvantage. I was not on staff at their bible school, and I had only briefly met most of them prior to their team trip. Neither had I been with them in Germany. So they had plenty of shared experiences, while I was something of an outsider. And then, suddenly, they were placed under the leadership of a relatively unknown person in a new place and a foreign culture.

As I pondered the question of how to bring about a good flow of relationships, Father God gave me an idea. It started with Paul's illustration of unity as the various parts of the body.[2] The idea was for us as a team to identify which body part each of us on the team represented. Who was the eyes (the visionary person)? Who was the ears (that most easily hear what the Lord is saying)? And so on.

This exercise wasn't about putting one another in boxes which would be limiting. Rather, it was about releasing identity which we hadn't necessarily

---

2. See 1 Cor 12:12–13

seen about ourselves. As identity was revealed, we grew together as a team. And peace was released among us.

Personality

Personality and identity are similar concepts, but they are not quite the same. Your personality is the visible aspect of your character; that is, your characteristics as an individual. Your personality embodies your interests, behaviors, habits, preferences, social and cultural traditions, and so on. Identity is the state of being yourself; that is, being what you are created to be.

Our personality traits may give a clue to our identity, but true identity goes much deeper.

For example, when I say that I am an American, I am describing an aspect of personality. Being an American is *not* my true identity. That doesn't mean that it is a bad thing to be an American. It simply means that my identity goes much deeper. I am convinced that Father God was intentional about having me grow up in America. But I am also convinced that my true identity encompasses being a child of the King in the Kingdom of Heaven.

For most of us, our experiences in life have led us to develop personality traits which may not quite be in tune with our true identity. Every step that we take to bring our personality into alignment with our true identity will increase the peace in our lives.

We may find ourselves trying to hide behind statements like: I am shy, I am an introvert, I am not very relational, I am . . . [whatever]. And we might have said those things to ourselves so many times that we assume them to be fact. And yet, your true identity is what Father God created you to be: A son or daughter in whom God Almighty is delighted, a prince or princess, the target of his love.

When God first met with Moses by the burning bush, he called himself "I AM." He didn't say, "I am good," or "I am love," or "I am holy." All of those things are true about him. But they are not his identity.

Identity is never based on what we do or how we behave. True identity is rooted in our very existence. It can't be changed by circumstances or any outward influence. But the things we encounter in life might cause our true identity to be hidden from us.

True Identity

Picnicking

When, on occasion, I begin to lose sight of my identity, I usually end up struggling. I may find myself struggling to be understood, or fighting to see my needs met. I might even describe it as a spiritual battle, where the enemy is out to steal and destroy those things which are mine.

But Father God has not created us to be warriors. We are created for love—created to be recipients of his love and created to respond in love. So when we feel as though we are overwhelmed by a battle, then we have moved outside of our true identity.

Psalm 23:5 tells us that Father God prepares a table before us in the presence of our enemies. In other words, a key to regaining our identity is found in picnicking. When we perceive that enemies are looming and feel as though we must struggle to get things to work out, Father God invites us on a picnic. He spreads a blanket, lays out a variety of choice morsels, and then sits down with us for a time of fellowship and pleasure. This is the nature of our God.

> Here I am! I stand at the door and knock. If anyone hears my voice
> and opens the door, I will come in and eat with that person, and
> they with me. (Rev 3:20)

In the context of this verse, Jesus has just revealed to a group of believers that they have been living in an illusion. They have actually no idea how completely out of touch they are with their true identity. They think of themselves as wealthy and insightful. But they are not.

Jesus is not angry with them. He is dissatisfied with their condition, because it hurts him to see them so destitute. They are not created to live this way. Their true identity is so much more!

And so Jesus, in his unfailing love for them, wants to reveal Truth to them. After pointing out the futility of the struggle, he says: What I really would like to do is come and eat a meal in fellowship with you. Let's talk about who you really are.

There is something significant about eating a meal in the presence of the Lord. Abraham ate lunch with the Living God (and two angels) prior to entering into an amazing dialog of intercession for the city of Sodom. And the entire system of feasts of worship, prescribed in the Law of Moses, centers around eating meals in the presence of the Lord. In this place of worship, fellowship, and pleasure we can easily experience a revelation of our true identity.

The Walk of the Child

In a healthy family setting, children eat most of their meals together with their parents. This is perhaps the primary context for learning who you are. It is around the table of fellowship that children learn what lies on the hearts of their parents. It is in this atmosphere of nurture and provision that a child becomes so much like their father—a chip off the old block.

Seen and Not Heard?

Perhaps you have heard the old adage that children should be seen and not heard. Perhaps you have even grown up under such a regime. Let me be very clear: It is a lie!

> Truly I tell you, unless you change and become like little children, you will never enter the kingdom of heaven. (Matt 18:3)

More than anything else, our true identity is that of a child. Before the creation, God was already Father. His primary purpose in creation was relational: to create sons and daughters for himself and a bride for his Son. We are created to be children.

There are some very important characteristics in the identity of a child.[3] A child trusts. A child does not worry. A child can be oblivious to the challenges surrounding them. A child plays. A child is filled with wonder. A child knows that their father can fix anything. A child has no experience with fear or abandonment. A child has nothing to prove. A child has no need of reputation. A child feels inherently safe. A child sees no limitations and believes that anything is possible. A child is at peace.

Burnout

In fact, I don't think I have ever heard of a child getting burned out. Burnout seems to be an adult thing. I am absolutely not an expert in psychology. But it seems to me that many people who find themselves facing burnout, have lost touch with their true identity as a beloved child of Father God.

Through the years, I have seen a number of people in ministry hit the wall. Usually, it is a consequence of trying to meet the expectations placed on them—placed either by their congregation or by themselves. We are not created to be crushed by expectations.

---

3. Of course, in a family situation which is less than ideal, these characteristics can be damaged over time. But that doesn't change the identity with which we are created.

True Identity

There is no burnout in the Kingdom of Heaven. It is the childlike at heart who find their place in that culture. A person with a childlike heart is free from the dominion of expectations. Such a heart answers only to the love of a Father who calls us beloved children in whom he is well pleased.

> Therefore, since we have been justified through faith, we have peace with God through our Lord Jesus Christ, through whom we have gained access by faith into this grace in which we now stand. And we boast in the hope of the glory of God. Not only so, but we also glory in our sufferings, because we know that suffering produces perseverance; perseverance, character; and character, hope. And hope does not put us to shame, because God's love has been poured out into our hearts through the Holy Spirit, who has been given to us. (Rom 5:1–5)

It is the love of Father God poured out into our hearts which is the source of peace. That love insulates us from external pressures (sufferings), gives us perspective (perseverance), shapes our identity (character), and fills us with joy (hope). The more we see our true identity, the less we are bound by the tyranny of maintaining a reputation. We may be misunderstood, ridiculed, or debased. But it doesn't matter when the love of God is poured out into our hearts.

And then, the more we walk in accordance with our true identity, the more we radiate a peace which releases and reveals to those around us their own true identity.

16

Health and Strength

DEUTERONOMY 7 TELLS ABOUT how the Lord God chose a people on whom he would pour out his love, and whom he wished to bring into a place of rest and peace. One of the conditions of this covenant of love was that they keep his commandments. One of the promises was that the Lord would keep them free from every disease.[1]

As we have seen earlier in this book, the old covenant gives an incomplete picture of the fullness that Father God has in store for us. When they entered into the promised land, they entered into an incomplete rest.[2] There is more to come. So, if the old covenant promised freedom from every disease, then freedom from every disease would be even more true under the new covenant.

And yet, we rarely see that.

Health and strength is probably the realm of peace with which I have the most limited experience. And that may be true for you as well. It is a somewhat sensitive subject. Much has been preached through the years, but not always from a perspective that brings peace.

The biggest challenge is the discrepancy between our experience with sickness, injuries and infirmities on the one hand, and God's promise of healing and freedom from sickness on the other. We see the theory, but it might not match our experience. Which often leaves us wondering why. And that is not a very peaceful place to be.

I don't know why.

---

1. See Deut 7:12–15
2. See Heb 3:7—4:11

I know that health and strength are the will of God for us. I know that there is no sickness in heaven. I know that Jesus taught us to pray for Father's will to be done on earth as in heaven. I know that people do get healed today—I have seen it happen. But I have also prayed earnestly for people and yet watched them die.

So we live in this place of mixture. And that place might make us feel uncomfortable. If it does, we could easily find ourselves trying to formulate a theology to explain the discrepancy. But the peacemaker should avoid doing so.

Deception

We can look a truth in the face, and yet not see it as a reality in our experience. And then, rather than trusting that Father God is in control and that he has a broader perspective than we can see, we look for a rational explanation. That can easily lead us into deception, where we find ourselves believing things which are not the Truth.

One very common falsehood is the thought that we don't see healing because of our lack of faith. It is possible to build a biblical case for such a thought, because Jesus did say on one occasion that the person's faith had healed them. But, making that one verse into a principle where I have to earn healing through the quality and/or quantity of my faith, is a serious distortion of the love of Father God. Healing is not a product of our efforts.

Another common lie is the idea that God brings sickness upon us in order to teach us something or to punish us for something. Again, it is possible to build a biblical case for this idea, especially in the context of old-covenant, knowledge of good and evil thinking. But that kind of thinking is no longer valid, thanks to the death of Jesus—by whose wounds we are healed.[3] Although it is entirely true that Father God can and does give us growth, insights and blessings through times of infirmity, I do not believe that sickness is ever his will or his doing.

Eliminating Chaos

One day, Jesus and three of his disciples had been on a mountain hike. When they came down again, they met a scene of chaos. There was a crowd,

---

3. See Isa 53:5

and the remaining disciples were in the midst of an argument with a bunch of religious leaders.

It turned out that the argument had to do with a young boy who was plagued by a spirit, with symptoms similar to what we might today call epilepsy. The disciples had been unable to help the boy. His desperate father was filled with doubt. The religious leaders were full of accusation. And the spirit was manifesting in the boy. It was not a peaceful scene.

When Jesus came, something changed. Jesus commanded the spirit to leave, and it did.

> After Jesus had gone indoors, his disciples asked him privately, "Why couldn't we drive it out?" He replied, "This kind can come out only by prayer." (Mark 9:28–29)

The Greek word *proseuchē*, translated here as prayer, implies a place of prayer or a state of earnestly praying. When we look at what Jesus did in this situation, it might be reasonable to interpret Jesus' answer something more like "This kind can only come out by changing the atmosphere so that peace, faith, and prayerfulness can prevail."[4]

When Jesus arrived, he put an end to the argument and silenced the words of unbelief. He took specific steps to end the chaos and to build faith. And then he commanded the spirit to leave.

If you look for it, you will see that this pattern of establishing peace and faith is found in several of the accounts where Jesus healed someone, such as the man who was born blind, the daughter of Jairus who was raised from the dead, and so on.

It is not a magic formula. But still, being a peacemaker, eliminating chaos, and fostering faith contribute to healing. This, I believe, is the kind of prayer Jesus spoke about.

The Heart of the Matter

> A heart at peace gives life to the body, but envy rots the bones. (Prov 14:30)

> A joyful heart causes good healing, but a broken spirit dries up the bones. (Prov 17:22 NASB with footnote)

---

4. My thanks to T M Leszko for introducing me to this observation, which he covers in greater detail in chapter 5 of his book *The New Covenant Fast*.

Health and Strength

Your well-being, and especially the well-being of your physical body, is closely related to the condition of your heart. The degree you walk in the realms of peace touched on in the previous chapters will influence your health and your strength. Living in fear, deception, dishonesty, anger, envy, insecurity, and so on creates an environment where sickness may flourish. Walking in trust, honesty, generosity, thankfulness, and security nourishes the body with health and strength.

Do not misunderstand me here. I am not saying that sickness is a consequence or punishment for you having wrong attitudes. Neither am I saying that there is a direct cause-and-effect relationship between a specific sickness and a specific behavior or attitude. Don't go down that road, because it only leads to accusation, shame, and guilt—none of which will lead to a heart at peace.

The point is that peace and joy contribute to an environment where health abounds.

In my own life, I am above average healthy. I don't get headaches, I am rarely ill, I am strong and moderately fit. At the same time, I do have a couple of chronic conditions that each require a certain level of attention and treatment. And yet, I refuse to let those conditions define who I am.

It seems that I do have some authority in the realm of headaches. Several times, I have felt like perhaps a headache was coming on, and then said, "Wait a second, here. I don't get headaches." Each time, the feeling of headache has gone away.

I once prayed for a woman who suffered from migraine headaches. When she came to me and explained her situation, the following words popped out of my mouth before I had a chance to think them through: "Is it your identity?" She answered with a definitive "No!" I prayed for her, and then she went home. Several months later, we crossed paths again and she told me what had happened that night. As she got into her car to drive home, she started to adjust the mirrors so that the reflection of bright lights would not bring on a migraine while she was driving. And then she recalled my question about identity and made the decision to no longer let the fear of migraine define her life. She told me that she had not had a headache since.

This is just one example of how a change of heart can bring change to the ecosystem of spirit, soul and body—and lead to good healing. But it is not a magic formula.

The Walk of the Child

A heart at peace is a good thing. What really matters is the love of the Father. And walking in peace gives more room for that love to express itself in our lives and in our physical bodies. As his love is poured out in our hearts, our experience of peace will expand.

17

The Tangible Presence of God

THE LORD JESUS IS described as the Prince of Peace, which leads me to conclude that peace reigns where he is. And he has told us that he is both at his Father's side and also always with us—because he and his Father dwell *in* us.[1]

Think about that. This enormous, powerful, amazing God has made his dwelling place in the hearts of his children. Which means that you, his beloved child, are *always* in his presence. You really can't come any closer to his presence than him dwelling in you.

But we may not always feel that way. In general, the degree to which I experience his presence is related to peace—especially how much my heart is at peace. Although there are occasions where the presence of God manifests visibly, for the most part his presence is expressed in love. God is love, and he has poured out his love into our hearts.[2] When we allow that love to fill us, there is no room for anything but love.

It is a bit of a chicken and egg kind of thing. His presence fills us with peace. And being at peace attracts his presence. He is always there, and yet there is more of him to experience. He is the fulfillment of peace, and yet it can still increase.

---

1. See Matt 28:20, Eph 1:20, John 14:23, and 1 John 4:15–16
2. See Rom 5:5

The Walk of the Child

Asylum

For nearly 20 years, we lived in a home in downtown Bergen, Norway—which is about three times as long as I have lived in any other home. That is a significant thing to me. Especially that I have been able to provide my children with a level of geographic stability which I did not experience in my own childhood.

But there's more.

The name of the street might best be translated as Asylum Place. Now, asylum is a word that might bring some unintended connotations so I would like to give you a definition. I have in my bookshelf a real treasure: a three-volume dictionary comprising nearly five thousand pages. This dictionary defines *asylum* as follows:

> I. A place of refuge and security.
>
> 1. Originally:
>
> A sanctuary, a place which it was deemed sacrilege for one to invade, and which, therefore, proved an inviolable retreat for criminals, debtors, and other people liable to be pursued.
>
> 2. Now:
>
> (a) Gen.: Any place of refuge: any place where one is sheltered, as a foreign land used as a retreat for political or religious refugees.
>
> (b) Spec.: An institution designed for the reception and shelter of those who are incapacitated from successfully fighting their own way in the world, as the blind asylum, the lunatic asylum.
>
> II. The protection accorded in such places; refuge, shelter.[3]

A definition like that, especially the original meaning of the word, resonates in a heart that is inclined toward peace. A place where our God chooses to dwell; the God who sends his blessings on the evil and the unrighteous as well as on the good and the righteous. A place where the presence of God is so tangible that even wicked people find safety in his holiness. What a place to be!

Historically, that street traces its name to the quarter-millennium-old building across the road, which once functioned as a children's shelter. It could be just a coincidence, but I rather choose to see the hand of

---

3. Hunter, *American Encyclopædic Dictionary*, 308

The Tangible Presence of God

God in history: Laying a foundation to build a heritage and a destiny for peace in my day.

In any case, through the years we have found ourselves, sometimes intentionally but perhaps even more often unintentionally, building up an environment of refuge in our home and in our neighborhood. In the intentional realm, we have prayed a hedge of protection. We have taken dominion over the space where we have authority. We have established a spiritual notice by the entrance which says, in effect, "check your demons at the door." In other words, things which are not conducive to peace are forbidden to invade or to violate the refuge of our home.

But such external forces are not really our focus. Rather, we are mostly intentional about maintaining a home environment that can be characterized as a resting place—for our many guests, for all who dwell in our home, and especially for the Lord who dwells in our midst.

Now don't misunderstand here. It's not as though we live in a monastery. There are still times of disagreement, there are children (and a husband) who can be rowdy or headstrong, there are occasions when one might say that we waste our time on quite ordinary things. But always with an eye to being a place of refuge.

Does it work?

For about fifteen years, a congregation of believers met in our home. Some came and went while others have been a part of the group for many years. One evening during our regular gathering, some unexpected guests arrived.

It was a young woman whom we knew, and who had been in and out of our home a bit. Although we (and many others) had invested in her, she was unable and/or unwilling to break free from the entanglement of drugs.

Anyhow, on this occasion she had three friends from that environment with her (her boyfriend, whom we had met, and two other men, whom we had never before seen). They came in during the teaching phase of our gathering, and the young woman fairly quickly became contentious. To be honest, the teaching wasn't that important, so we changed course. But the boyfriend was embarrassed by his girlfriend's behavior. So the couple left, leaving the two men behind.

We ended up spending the next couple of hours just chatting and drinking coffee with these two men. It turned out they were both pretty heavy addicts, having been on the needle for decades. And they were also a bit embarrassed about being there—they had no idea they were being brought to a private home. That evening they had an experience of the peace of God's tangible presence. It's not that we saw them get saved or delivered from their addiction that evening, but there was still a powerful testimony of their experience of peace, when one of them said, "Have I really been here for more than two hours? I don't think I've gone so long without a smoke in 30 years!"

Peacefully Longing for More

People often tell us that they feel there is such a peace in our house. They don't always have the vocabulary for it, but it is obvious to us that they are experiencing the presence of God. We once had a guest who stayed a couple of nights in our basement family room. He insisted that there was really good air in that basement, because he hadn't slept so well in years.[4]

Which may leave you wondering: What's it like to live in that? How do you make it happen?

To be honest, I'm not really sure how to answer that. We have lived it 24/7, so it seems fairly normal to us. And perhaps it should be *normal* to live in the peace of God. We have a lifestyle that includes a lot of worship, fellowship, and hospitality. Those things contribute to making a resting place for the presence of God. We also do not have a television, which might help a bit. But more than anything else, there is a huge amount of the grace of God. He is really, really good. And we benefit from that.

Before you get the wrong idea, I want to reiterate. We are not super-spiritual. We are fairly ordinary people living in a fairly ordinary home. We don't hold all night prayer vigils calling for the Lord's visitation. We live out our daily lives in peace. And though we do experience some degree of the tangible presence of God, there is much more available.

It might be possible to call down more. Or it might be possible to become so much more childlike that his tangible presence simply lands. I don't know of any formula for making it happen. There probably isn't one.

More than a hundred years ago, in an abandoned church building in an insignificant suburb of Los Angeles, a group of very ordinary people started gathering to pray. Some of them prayed a lot. And something happened. For reasons known only to Father God, his tangible presence was manifested in an unusually powerful way.

---

4. It's a basement. The air isn't all that good down there. But those were his words to describe his experience.

The Tangible Presence of God

For more than three years there was a visible cloud of the presence of God in that building on Azusa Street. Sometimes it was just a mist along the floor, while at other times it was a thick cloud. On occasion the children there even played hide-and-seek in the cloud! And on more than one occasion, the fire department was called out because it seemed as though the building was engulfed in flames.

I dream about experiencing that level of the tangible presence of God. Not because I want to have a good story to tell or because I want to repeat something from revival history. But because I want to be overwhelmed by him.

Conclusion

Blessed are the peacemakers, for they will be called children of God.
(MATT 5:9)

ALTHOUGH YOU MIGHT HAVE forgotten it along the way, this is a book about sonship. In a healthy family setting, a son or daughter reflects the nature and character of their father.

It is not enough, for those whose desire is to delight Father God, to live a life within the boundaries of the biblical commands. That is the behavior of servants.[1] A true son or daughter has their heart set on being like their father. Or, looking to the example of Jesus, a true son or daughter does what they see Father doing and speaks what they hear Father speaking.

Jacob and Esau

Isaac, the son of Abraham, had two sons who were twins. Even before they were born, it was prophesied that the older would serve the younger. And it was later said that Jacob had God's favor while Esau did not.[2] Which leaves me wondering: Why? There is a verse which I suspect gives a clue:

> When the boys grew up, Esau became a skillful hunter, a man of the field, but Jacob was a peaceful man, living in tents. (Gen 25:27 NASB)

---

1. See Luke 17:10
2. See Gen 25:22–23, Mal 1:2–3 and Rom 9:13.

Conclusion

This verse is the first description of the twins after their birth. The word translated *peaceful* here[3] is the Hebrew word *tam*. It means perfect, complete, lacking nothing; sound, wholesome, quiet; morally innocent, having integrity.

The comparison is interesting. Esau is described as a hunter, an activity which would require aggression and a measure of violence. And Jacob, by contrast, is described as peaceful. As their story continues, Jacob builds a relationship of trust and open communication with God, while Esau does not.

One of the fascinating, but perhaps confusing, aspects of the story is that Jacob was *not* always a model of righteous behavior. He was at times deceitful and manipulative. His swindle of Esau's birthright and blessing were far from good examples of how brothers should relate to one another. So, from a knowledge of good and evil perspective, the story of God's blessing on Jacob's life is difficult to understand.

But it is not the nature of our Good Father to see things from that perspective. Throughout his life, Jacob moved into an increasing revelation of God as his Father, and he learned to know the heart of God. In other words: Blessed was Jacob, the peaceful man, who became known as a son of God.

Sometimes It Gets Messy

It was my wife's birthday. The plan was to celebrate with a family breakfast. So I was to start the day by making a batch of Alaska Sourdough Pancakes—a Sunday morning tradition in our home.

When I came into the kitchen, I was surprised to find our daughter and our not quite three-year-old granddaughter. Our granddaughter insisted that, if we were going to celebrate a birthday, then there needed to be a cake. So they were going to make one. And I walked in just as they had learned the lesson that eggs break when you drop them on the table.

Well, with a two-year-old involved, the process took much longer than necessary. Ingredients were wasted. A mess was made. And the end result wasn't all that pretty. But, thanks to plenty of sugar, it tasted fine. And *Mormor*,[4] who had been banished from the kitchen due to the secret project, was completely charmed and delighted.

It's usually a lot like that when we think we are helping Father God. We don't necessarily do things in the best, most effective, or right way, and

---

3. Other translations render it as plain, quiet, or content
4. Norwegian for Grandma

we frequently end up making a mess of it all. Even so, he is delighted to be doing things together with us. Because, for the most part, the results *really do not matter*! If Father simply wants something to get done, he has plenty of serving angels to do it for him. But in the delight of Father and son or daughter doing things together, it is the time and the process that matters. Father wants the relationship, the heart-to-heart communication, and the experience of the road walked hand in hand.

Jonah

The prophet Jonah's story is like that. It is primarily a sonship story. That may surprise you.

In a nutshell, the Sunday School version of Jonah's story goes something like this: God told Jonah to go to Nineveh and prophesy. Jonah didn't want to, so he tried to run away. But God sent a storm, Jonah got thrown in the sea, and a big fish swallowed him. After three days, the fish burped Jonah on to land, and he ended up having to go to Nineveh after all. Which might lead us to conclude: You had better do as God says, because you can't run away from him.

But there is a lot more to the Jonah story than a big fish as a punishment for disobedience.

First off, if God was primarily concerned with getting his message delivered to Nineveh, then he could have simply asked another person after Jonah ran away. The fact that God used such extraordinary measures to include Jonah in the story makes it clear that God's purposes went far beyond delivering a message.

Next, there is the reason why Jonah ran away:

> Isn't this what I said, LORD, when I was still at home? That is what I tried to forestall by fleeing to Tarshish. I knew that you are a gracious and compassionate God, slow to anger and abounding in love, a God who relents from sending calamity. (Jonah 4:2)

Jonah was angry with God, because God had shown mercy. The message which Jonah had been asked to deliver to Nineveh was that God planned to bring disaster on the city because of their evil ways. Both Jonah and God understood that the people of Nineveh would respond to the message and change their ways, thereby leading God to relent from bringing destruction. So Jonah had tried to circumvent that result by running away.

(He might also have known prophetically that their descendants would one day destroy Israel.)

The problem was that God delights in showing mercy,[5] while Jonah did not. And that bothered God. He really wanted Jonah, his son, to learn of his ways and to share in the desires of his heart. Despite Jonah's disobedience and his stubborn attitude, God did not get angry with or punish Jonah. Rather, he demonstrated his love toward Jonah. True love is contagious, and God wanted Jonah to be smitten.

First Love

> But I have this against you, that you have left your first love. Therefore remember from where you have fallen, and repent and do the deeds you did at first (Rev 2:4–5a)

Often, I have heard this verse preached or exhorted as something of an accusation—implying that I somehow should make myself more passionate in my love.

One day, I felt as if Father asked me, "What does first love look like?" Good question, I thought. I would guess that most of us picture the concept of first love as being something like infatuation—that feeling of being head over heels in love. Perhaps something like that first time you had a crush on someone at school.

But then Father asked, "What was the first love you experienced?" And the answer to that, though I don't consciously remember it, was the love I received as an infant.

Think about it. I kept my parents awake, I spit on their clothes, I filled diapers and generally made a mess. I didn't do anything useful, but instead selfishly demanded food and attention, at both the best and worst of times. And yet, I was loved!

In light of all that, what does it mean to return to your first love and to do those first deeds? I hope you will agree that it does not mean returning to the behavior of a selfish and helpless infant.

But I think it does mean reclaiming that state of being unconditionally loved. It means no longer doing things in order to be good enough. It means actively living in acceptance and wholeness independent of what I may or may not do to deserve it. It means being dependent on Father and

---

5. See Mic 7:18

being connected to his heart and his ways. It means eating from the Tree of Life and no longer thinking in terms of good and evil. First love is really all about *receiving* the Father's love!

It seems to me this is what God was trying to say to Jonah. Jonah was loved, both before and after the fish, both before and after his temper tantrum on the slope outside of Nineveh, whether or not he understood what God was up to. But God wasn't satisfied to leave Jonah steeping in his anger and disappointment. God wanted to train up a world changer. And that starts with peace. When we carry the Kingdom of Peace in our lives, it changes our surroundings and peace breaks out.

Discipling Nations

Jesus, in what is often called The Great Commission,[6] called us to make disciples of all nations. That is frequently interpreted to mean that we should disciple some people from every nation. Which is true. But I believe it also means that each of us should live in such a way that we *disciple* the nation in which we live. By that, I mean that our lifestyle should influence our culture to become more like the culture in the Kingdom of Heaven. And that kingdom is ruled by the Prince of Peace. The role of the peacemaker is essential in discipling a nation.

> I urge, then, first of all, that petitions, prayers, intercession and thanksgiving be made for all people—for kings and all those in authority, that we may live peaceful and quiet lives in all godliness and holiness. (1 Tim 2:1–2)

Paul wrote these words in a far more savage culture than most of us in modern Western society have experienced. Many gods were worshiped, and those gods (whom Paul described as demons[7]) craved sacrifice—preferably human sacrifice. There were the blatant sacrifices of parents who "passed their children through the fire." But there were also the less obvious sacrifices of public executions, gladiator fights, and warfare. That kind of worship empowers demonic influence in society.[8] Which, in turn, leads to

---

6. See Matt 28:18–20
7. See 1 Cor 10:20
8. See 2 Kgs 3:26–27 and Isa 33:14–17

Conclusion

a society where people feast their eyes on evil and entertain themselves with human death. This makes fertile ground for persecution of Christians.[9]

Against this backdrop, Paul urged that we pray in every possible manner for all people, and especially those who govern—with a very specific goal: A peaceful society. Without doubt, the ways of peace are powerful for reversing the demonic influence in society. The people Paul urges us to pray for are not necessarily good people. They may, in fact, be quite evil. And yet Paul urges us to pray *for* them—not against them, not as if they were enemies—but for them.

This is what sets our God apart from other gods. There are other religions where the god is professed to be a god of love. But our God loves his enemies, blesses those who don't deserve it, turns the other cheek, and defeats evil through weakness and foolishness.

It took a few centuries of persecution, suffering, and martyrdom before this weakness toppled the idolatry of the Roman Empire. Today, at least in most Western democracies, we see so little persecution and martyrdom that we live in the illusion that a peaceful society is normal. But it is not. Unless the children of Father God actively and visibly live as peacemakers in their society, the peace to which we have become so accustomed will evaporate. And our cultures will lose sight of the revelation of the God of Peace. We already see our cultures moving in that direction. But do we respond as peacemakers? Are we meeting the challenge? Are we walking into The Call of the Child?

Peace is not about right and wrong. It is inherent in the nature of peacemaking that peace be freely offered to those who do not deserve it, and who might not respond in kind. Anything less than that is less than true peace.[10]

The Blessing of Peace

In our look at the history of punishment in chapter 1, we saw a pattern of covenant woven through the history of God's dealing with mankind. Each new covenant revealed something more of the nature of God. But even more importantly, each new covenant was a step toward achieving the purpose of the Lord set out before the foundation of the world: A Father

---

9. For a good portrayal of what this looked like in the third century, I recommend the historical novel, *Perpetua* by Amy Peterson.

10. See Matt 5:46–47

who longs to raise up children for himself and a bride for his Son. This is perhaps expressed most clearly in the new covenant prophesied by Ezekiel:

> I will give you a new heart and put a new spirit in you; I will remove from you your heart of stone and give you a heart of flesh. And I will put my Spirit in you and move you to follow my decrees and be careful to keep my laws. (Ezek 36:26–27)

Ezekiel describes this new covenant as a heart transplant, and goes on to describe how it works. Father God takes away the heart that is bound to follow commandments written on stone tablets. (This, I believe, is the death of the old man in baptism.) And he replaces it with a living heart, a heart of flesh which eats of the Tree of Life. He fills us with his Spirit and his Spirit in us *moves* us to walk in his ways.

In this covenant we no longer strive to do what is right. Rather, the love of God which is poured into our hearts[11] moves us to walk in his ways without effort. This is the place of peace.

This love is not just a concept, but a tangible and very real substance. When you fill a glass with water, there is no room for any air. When a person is filled with the love of God, there is no room for any sin. Love is transferred through the lover's gaze on their beloved. It originates in the Father—the child need only receive. And Father God is Love. He is the original and the ultimate lover. To be in this place of peace is The Call of the Child.

In his final talk with his disciples, prior to his crucifixion, Jesus put it this way: "I have told you these things, so that in me you may have peace."[12] What were these things that he told them? That the Father loves them. That this love is a direct line of communication, so they no longer need to relate to the Father through any mediator. That the Spirit of Truth will fill them with the presence of the Father and of the Son so that they will never be alone. That they will be filled with peace. This is the blessing of the Father.

> The LORD bless you and keep you; the LORD make his face shine on you and be gracious to you; the LORD turn his face toward you and give you peace. (Num 6:24–26)

---

11. See Rom 5:5
12. John 16:33a

Bibliography

Alexander, Harriet. "How Mexico's most dangerous city transformed itself to become safe enough for the Pope." *The Telegraph* (February 17, 2016). https://www.telegraph.co.uk/news/worldnews/centralamericaandthecaribbean/mexico/12155890/How-Mexicos-most-dangerous-city-transformed-itself-to-become-safe-enough-for-the-Pope.html retrieved Oct 16, 2020.
Bos, Pieter. *The Nations Called*. Kent: Sovereign World, 2002.
Burk, Arthur. *The Redemptive Gifts of Cities*. Audio teaching from Sapphire Leadership Group, 2004.
Egeberg, Kristoffer. "Ti politimenn drept siden krigen." Oslo: *Dagbladet* (Mar 4, 2010). https://www.dagbladet.no/nyheter/ti-politimenn-drept-siden-krigen/64982491 retrieved Oct 16, 2020.
Galpin, Trevor. *The Story of Paul: The Early Years*. Suffolk, VA: TLG Mins, 2018.
Hunter, Robert, ed. *The American Encyclopædic Dictionary*. Chicago, IL: Ogilvie, 1894.
Jordan, M. James. *The Ancient Road Rediscovered: What the Early Church Knew*. Taupo: Fatherheart Media, 2014.
Karlsson, Pelle. *Korsets Princip*. Stockholm: Förlaget Filadelfia, 1983.
Leszko, T. M. *The New Covenant Fast*. Merging Streams, 2017.
Levitsky, Steven and Daniel Ziblatt. *How Democracies Die: What History Reveals About our Future*. London: Penguin, 2019.
Lewis, C. S. *The Screwtape Letters*. New York: HarperCollins, 1942, 1961, 1996.
Lindberg, Per, Ørjan Torheim and Marianne Nilsen. "På 16 måneder er tre menn skutt og drept av politiet". Bergens Tidende. (January 6, 2021). https://www.bt.no/nyheter/lokalt/i/JJ6qnm/paa-16-maaneder-er-tre-menn-skutt-og-drept-av-politiet retrieved Jan 9, 2021.
McKibben, Bruce. *Walking His Ways*. Bergen: Independently published, 2018.
National Law Enforcement Officers Memorial Fund. "Officer Deaths by Year." https://nleomf.org/facts-figures/officer-deaths-by-year retrieved Oct 16, 2020.
Peterson, Amy Rachel. *Perpetua: A Bride, A Martyr, A Passion*. Orlando, FL: Relevant, 2004.
Philpott, Daniel, and Timothy Samuel Shah, eds. *Under Ceasar's Sword: How Christians Respond to Persecution*. Cambridge: Cambridge University Press, 2019.
Silvoso, Ed. *Ekklesia: Rediscovering God's Instrument for Global Transformation*. Ada, MI: Chosen Books, 2017.
———. *Transformation: Change the Marketplace and You Change the World*. Ventura, CA: Regal Books, 2007.

Bibliography

Wikipedia. "List of countries by firearm-related death rate." Wikipedia. https://en.wikipedia.org/wiki/List_of_countries_by_firearm-related_death_rate retrieved Oct 16, 2020.

———. "List of killings by law enforcement officers by country." Wikipedia. https://en.wikipedia.org/wiki/List_of_killings_by_law_enforcement_officers_by_country retrieved Oct 16, 2020.

———. "Small Arms Survey." Wikipedia. https://en.wikipedia.org/wiki/Small_Arms_Survey retrieved Oct 16, 2020.

www.ingramcontent.com/pod-product-compliance
Lightning Source LLC
Chambersburg PA
CBHW072134160426
43197CB00012B/2108